PlusOne = 3

No relationship is straightforward
This one came with an assignment

Sonia Harris

ISBN.13: 978-1-983118-01-2

Cover design by Tiny Designs Ltd

Printed in the United Kingdom

CONTENTS

FOREWORD

Reading through this manuscript, there is nothing that I didn't already know. However, recounting and recalling parts of our journey together, I was hooked. Each chapter had me looking forward to what was coming next with anticipation. It was a sharp reminder of how my (and our) actions have had a direct impact on the life of others, positively as well as negatively. Allowing God into this process has moved us from one level to another. Sonia's journey before me has become me – and it has culminated in who we are now, but also where we are going. This book has offered me the opportunity for reflection, to see how far we have come, and insight into what He has in store for us.

When Sonia informed me that she was going to write this book, I knew she would see it through to the end – no matter how long it took. Incredibly, she has managed to complete it in the timeframe she set, despite work, motherhood, ministry, mentoring and ME!

I have often said, in jest and sometimes in frustration, that Sonia is like 'a dog with a bone'. Reading through this book has helped me to understand why.

'Mrs Harris' you are amazing, and I am inspired by who you are with the additional aspect of what you do…. Love you!

Rob Harris

ACKNOWLEDGEMENTS

It would be wrong, and frankly rude of me to not acknowledge and thank those that have been an integral part of this book, but more importantly my life.

Rob – next to the word 'patience' in the dictionary is a picture of you. Not quite smiling, but there you are. Thank you for waiting for me to become the wife you prayed for. Don't stop praying!

To our beautiful boys; Tye, a mini, male version of me. I get it, son. Dain, who never stops moving but knows how to move - watch this space. Campbell, you have taught me to see a different perspective. I love you all. You make me the mother I am. 1-2-3 Team Harris!

Mum, you set the standards and gave me the template to work with. I will forever be grateful for the sacrifices.

Skint, you pulled me up when I went too far and then you turned me into a lady. Only with you can I laugh until words are not possible. I miss you.

My brothers, even from afar I felt protected and precious. Thank you.

Pats, perfectionism starts and ends with you. Thank you for the example.

Pastor Steve, you opened your house and your home to me when I was fatherless. You guided me when I was lost and spoke the truth when I didn't want to hear it. Few words mean so much when the heart is right. Thank you for the investment.

Julia, you told me to focus on one verse at a time. The verses came together to form chapters. Thank you.

Dad, you passed down your humour and mischievousness and I got it. I miss the roasted chestnuts but not the heat. Sleep well.

Uncle Fruits, not a day goes by without me eating fruit, but the mangoes are reserved for you. See you soon.

Phil, you led the way and prayed without ceasing. God bless you and your beautiful family.

Jen, you told me to keep writing even when I didn't know how. You told me it wasn't my fault. You released me. I'll never forget it.

Sam, you witnessed without words and remained true to yourself. You were the vessel, you were my guide. You shared your home (church) with me and put the bible in my hands. Eternally grateful.

To Auntie Beatrice, who prayed and fasted with me until God delivered. Thank you for your obedience, your example and your faith!

To Ruth, you thought that ticket was for Jos. God had another plan. Thank you for your guidance and input. You were right, I can't plan EVERYTHING!

To my Godson (E) – Beautiful inside and out. You reassure me that it's possible. I pray my sons will follow your example. Never stop searching.

Bev, you told me to 'check myself'. I didn't like it, but I did it, eventually. Your words have become my words. Thank you for your honesty and obedience.

Juliet - my sounding board. You keep it real and you encourage me to be better. We share the same passion and that keeps us on the same path – even if it means enormous amounts of mileage. There for you Miss B.

To Frances (Sis), you enable us to do what we do. Your heart is huge. Thank you for your support and sacrifice.

Marcia, you gave me the unspoken permission to be real and honest without tearing down. You showed me marriage through another lens. Crockery every time!

To Bunmi, a fellow author. Thank you for taking the time to explain it to me.

To my church family – you encourage me and keep me moving forward. Every encouraging word goes in and energises me for the next step.

To Sipho, who read the first draft in record time. Thank you for your time, investment and honesty. You keep me on my toes – I know you're watching!

To my girls (too many to name, you know who you are) – You warm my heart as I see you grow and expand into what God has for you. I'm never too busy!

To those couples we take pleasure in spending time with. You trust us – you teach us.

To you – thank you for your time. I can't return it to you, but I hope you'll find that it's time well spent.

1 INTRODUCTION

"Share it."

As we stood with our Pastor, silent, having just explained that we believed that God had called us to be together, we waited.

We had arranged to meet with Pastor Steve following the evening service.

Honestly, I hadn't heard a word of the sermon that evening.

My focus had been on the meeting which was to follow the service and now that the service was over the meeting was drawing ever closer.

As we waited for other church members and guests to conclude their conversations, (there were many, too many) we edged closer and closer until we were beckoned over to some chairs that were vacant.

I realized, quickly, that we were going to do this, right here!

No private office.

Not even a corridor!

Right here in front of others.

The fact that no-one could hear what was being said was only mildly comforting.

We sat, in a row, with our Pastor sat between us.

He leaned back in the seat with both arms stretched wide, resting on the backs of our seats, one leg crossed over the other - a comfortable position, indicating to me that he was not concerned about what he was about to hear.

I, however, was leaning forward in my seat only occupying the front half of the seat pad, both feet firmly planted on the floor.

I glanced at Rob.

Whilst he too was leaning forward and had turned towards me, he was looking remarkably calm and together.

He gave me a reassuring semi-smile and his eyes narrowed just a little.

I knew that look already.

Despite the fact that we had only been dating for two weeks, I was learning his unspoken language quickly.

Rob is a wise, contemplative man.

He is very good at expressing himself but doesn't speak just for the sake of it.

He will often use an expression when words are not required.

This was one of those times - and it was enough.

I relaxed a little.

Just a little.

My nerves were justified. I had been here once before.

Sort of.

Not in the same capacity.

It hadn't ended well - but that's another story!

Needless to say, I didn't want the same outcome.

Rob was calm.

Rob is always calm - mostly.

Rob has a relaxed, reassuring spirit that pretty much follows him wherever he goes.

It had certainly followed him to this meeting!

Pastor Steve had a knowing smile on his face.

Almost a smirk - but not quite.

He knew what we were about to tell him.

He always knew.

Not much surprised him.

I had already decided that Rob would do the talking.

Ordinarily, I would be the mouthpiece - happy to give my opinion on any subject at any time and ready to talk until daybreak.

Rob, on the other hand, whilst happy to engage in conversation, would tend to listen and observe and then contribute something profound.

I had already come to admire that about him.

Rob started to speak, and I found myself holding my breath.

As Rob continued, Pastor Steve changed stance. He leaned forward in his seat, both feet on the floor, elbows on knees, hands together, fingers entwined.

He tapped one foot, 1-2-3.

Rob stopped talking.

Pastor Steve had heard enough.

He sat up straight, and on an outward breath said, "This is great!"

He stood to his feet indicating that the meeting was over.

I exhaled and jumped up onto my feet.

Rob stood in slow motion. He looked at me, his eyes were shining.

Pastor Steve placed an arm around each of us - me on his right, Rob on his left, and as we stood, heads down, in this forward-facing embrace feeling like we had just been ordained by the Queen herself, Pastor Steve spoke the words that would remain with us for a very long time to come, *"Share it!"*

And there began our future....... or so we thought!

We soon came to realise that our future together had started long before that moment.

2 THE END FROM THE BEGINNING

As you delve deeper into the pages of this book you will discover more about the history of our relationship, both with each other and with Christ.

You will also discover more about our singleness and our upbringing.

We often share about our past because we have been instructed to - by God and by our shepherd.

You will discover many similarities between us, but also many differences.

Oh, we are very different.

In many ways.

For instance, I am proactive, Rob is reactive.

I plan everything well in advance and am like a dog with a bone (Rob`s words, not mine) once an idea comes into my head.

Rob deals with the issue as it arises, gets the job done and moves on to the next task.

We both `produce the goods` but we have a different method and approach.

Neither is wrong or right but side by side, it can cause friction.

Now, God our creator knows this about us. Of course, He does - he created us to be this way and this goes some way towards explaining our journey towards Him and each other.

In brief, Rob had an encounter with the Lord one night when he believed his life was in danger and in the midst of a car chase he said the words, 'God if you are real, get me out of this alive and I'll commit my life to you!'

God did - and he did!

I, on the other hand, experienced a more thought-through process.

For a good two years, prior to giving my life to Christ, a very close friend of mine who had already committed his life to Christ had been trying to speak to me about making a commitment myself.

I wasn't interested.

In fact, I made every effort to avoid him.

His life had been so transformed that I didn't feel that I knew him personally anymore.

In fact, his commitment to Christ had left me feeling very alone and I began to resent Christianity for taking him away from me.

We had been friends for many, many years and he had become the brother I never had.

Don't get me wrong, I have brothers - 3 in fact! But they are all much older than me and I didn't really grow up with them - they left the family home before I was old enough to remember.

So, there I was, feeling like there was a huge gap left by the absence of my friend.

I began to ponder the meaning of life.

Everything was going in circles with no end goal.

I remember having the growing desire to do good things, acts of kindness, but not knowing how to execute that feeling.

At one point, I remember having the desire to walk elderly or blind people across the road!

I felt that that would give me a sense of `doing good`.

In fact, one morning, on the way to work, as I arrived at my local train station, a blind man asked me if I wouldn't mind assisting him to the train platform as the trains were departing from alternative platforms that day - I can't recall why.

I was delighted.

As this man took my elbow and trusted me to get him safely to the alternative platform I had such a sense of fulfilment and purpose.

I liked it!

Nothing much happened after that, but I could feel myself changing.

I was beginning to desire more from life.

One thing that was really beginning to bother me, however, was the overriding sense of being alone.

It would seem as if everyone had something to do, somewhere to go or someone to be with - especially at the weekends.

Ironically, at the weekends, I would often take myself off to IKEA in Wembley.

It was the only place I knew how to get to by car that was far enough away to feel like a day trip.

I was, and still am, terrible with directions. I mean, really bad.

Back then, I had no Sat Nav or Google maps on my mobile phone!

It was the printed A-Z road atlas or nothing.

So, I would often frequent IKEA in Wembley and spend the afternoon strolling through the showroom and the market place pretending to be looking for items to furnish my 'place'.

I'd buy nothing!

I couldn't afford to buy anything - I just needed somewhere to go.

Who knows that the one place you will certainly find couples, all looking loved up and planning for their future is IKEA!!!

And yet, there I would be, alone, almost weekly.

At this stage I was getting into my late 20`s and my mind was starting to focus on getting into a relationship that would build towards my future.

I had no problem with being single.

In fact, I had had enough relationships in the past to not want to bother with yet another one that would inevitably end in two to three months.

All the others had.

If I'm honest, I couldn't see myself being married for the rest of my life.

My parents hadn't managed it and neither had my friends parents - all bar one.

I remember vividly, whilst I was still at school, a group of friends and I had had one of *those* conversations where we asked, "Who do you think will be the first to get married?"

One of my friends responded quickly, "Sonia!"

Quickly followed by, "But she'll be the first to get divorced too!"

We all laughed - and I believed it! I really did.

I had no examples around me to prove otherwise and my relationship track record was evidence to back it up!

One thing I was confident about was my desire to be a mother.

I was in no rush for that to happen, mind you, but I knew I wanted to be a mother someday.

I also knew that I wanted to be married before having children.

The confusion within me was, 'If I can't see myself staying married but I want to have children I would have to prepare myself to be a single mother at some point.'

I mean, no-one plans to be a single mother, do they?

It happens, but you don't start out thinking it will be that way, do you?

Well, I did.

As it happens, when I was 18 years of age, I bought my first house.

Now, let's stop there for a moment!

There are a number of factors that led up to me buying a property at such a young age, but ultimately part of my parents' divorce agreement was that the family home was to be sold when the youngest child from the marriage turned 17.

That was me.

I was the youngest.

And, without ever speaking it aloud, I felt this unspoken pressure to grow up, fast, so that my parents could be released from the one thing that was binding them together.

My parents' divorce was extremely bitter. They wanted nothing to do with each other, and, if I remember rightly, they started the process of divorce when I was about 5 years old.

So, as you can imagine, this was a very long, drawn out process.

One thing led to another, and certain avenues led nowhere, and so here I was, buying a property so that I had somewhere to live when my mother pursued her dream of retiring back to the Caribbean.

Now, my mother is a strong, responsible, caring woman.

A prayerful woman, who loves her children and sacrificed so much to ensure we were provided for.

In my heart, even at that young age, I appreciated all that she had done to give us a comfortable life.

She made sacrifices and fought hard to keep us safe, warm, fed etc.

I knew, without a doubt, that it was time for her to live her life now and enjoy however many years she had left.

With that in mind, I knew my mother would only have true peace if she knew that we were all settled, safe and secure.

My decision to purchase the house I grew up in was a major factor in giving her peace of mind.

But, it came at a price.

Again, she sacrificed, this time her share of the sale of the property, so that I would have a good start in life.

For that I will always be thankful.

So, now, I had a 3-bedroomed terraced house in East London and in the back of my mind was this sense of security, that if I got married and then divorced (this had now become my life plan) I would raise my children in this home.

You remember I mentioned that I am a planner.

This is an example of how my mind works!

This plan became embedded and coupled with the rejection I had received from my father when I was 13 years old, my view of relationships, commitment, trust, loyalty, love and all the other factors that contribute to a healthy marriage was becoming very, very warped.

Let's return to my journey to Christ.

After sensing a change within, but not knowing it was a call to Christ, I continued to function as `normal`.

I lived alone and so would leave and return to an empty home each day.

Mostly, this did not bother me too much, but I was beginning to feel more and more empty.

I would journey to and from work each day and would meet with friends etc but on the whole I would spend a lot of time alone.

One Friday evening, returning from work, I was feeling really low.

I arrived at my flat and as I closed the front door, I leaned against it and didn't move for a while.

Ordinarily I would turn on the lights, turn on the TV, get myself changed out of my work attire and into something more comfortable, settling in for the evening.

But this evening was different.

I walked slowly to my bed and sat on the end of it, facing the window which looked out onto the busy street.

I stared out of the window, seeing nothing.

I just sat there.

For ages.

Coat and shoes on.

Just sat there.

And then, I started to cry.

And I couldn't stop.

Anyone who knew me at that time would tell you, this was not something I would do.

I very rarely cried, and if I did it was out of anger or frustration. It was never sorrowful, like it was at that moment.

The only other thing I remembered that evening was tipping to the right and lying on my bed, feet still on the floor, and the crying continued.

Deep, wrenching, sorrowful sobbing.

When I woke up it was morning.

I was still in the same position!

I sat up slowly and took in what had happened over the last 10 hours or so and I began to cry all over again.

My body ached.

I still had my coat and shoes on from the night before and I felt pitiful.

I hadn't eaten.

I didn't want to.

I didn't want to move. I just sat there and cried. I was no longer sobbing – tears just fell.

Around midday I received this overwhelming feeling to be in a church! I had no idea why. I hadn't been to church for so long.

My mother is a Catholic and she would take my sister and I to church every week without fail until we became teenagers and began to continually make excuses as to why we couldn't come along. After a while she gave up and let us stay home (in bed) on a Sunday morning as long as we did our chores and cooked the dinner before she got home.

Deal!

Now, in this moment, I recalled that there was a church across the road from where I lived, and I quickly got myself ready to go. There was an urgency to get there. I had planned to go shopping with my sister that afternoon, but I called to cancel. I tried my best to make my croaky voice sound normal on the phone, but my sister knows me too well. She sensed something was up. I had to plead with her not to come over, explaining that I just needed some time and would touch base with her later.

As I crossed over the road and sheepishly entered the church I felt a sense of peace and calm. But, as I sat in the empty, wooden pews, looking up at the hanging crucifix above me, I still felt something was missing. I couldn't put my finger on it, but something just didn't feel right.

I continued to sit, looking at Jesus - blood dripping from his wounds.

My tears were still falling. My head was sore, my eyes swollen.

I felt weak. And empty.

A small choir started to assemble over in the far right corner; I assumed they were rehearsing for mass the next day. They didn't focus on me, but I felt self-conscious sitting there, alone, crying.

Whilst it may not have been unusual for them to see someone doing this, for me, it was completely alien and really quite uncomfortable.

I usually had it all together - or so I would have everyone think.

As the choir sang hymns, my mind started to unravel stored information.

Sam!

Sam was a friend I had met about a year before.

We had become friends through mutual friends - a friend of a friend of a friend! He would come and visit me at home every week or so.

Occasionally we would go to a gig or to watch a movie but generally he would come over to my place and just hang out.

Sam was different.

Different to other guys I knew. He would come over, have a cup of tea, maybe a sandwich (Sam always teased that I didn't have much in my fridge) and we'd watch a documentary. Then he'd leave to go home.

I knew Sam went to church. He'd told me that as soon as I'd met him.

I also knew he played the bass guitar.

Sam loved his bass. He would handle it tenderly and with so much care. I would tease him that his bass was his wife!

At that moment, sitting in that church, crying, I remembered Sam.

I realised what was missing as I sat there, in this church, waiting.

I couldn't put words to it, but I felt that Sam`s church would have it.

I jumped up and rushed out of that church and caught a bus into town.

I was still crying but my shoulders had dropped a little. Now, instead of tension, I felt anticipation and a little excitement mixed with apprehension.

With this cocktail of emotions racing through my body my stomach felt like it was in knots.

The bus journey was taking too long! It had arrived quickly enough to pick me up, but it was stopping too often, delaying me from my destination.

It was Saturday afternoon and people were busy with shopping and children.

I took this bus to town regularly. I knew the route, but today it was taking forever to get me to where I needed to be. I became agitated and anxious at the same time.

I'd never been to Sam's church before, but I was excited at what I might find.

As I arrived in town and exited the bus I realised I wasn't even sure where Sam`s church was. I knew roughly. He'd told me once when we first met. I recalled that information now and quickly found the building.

I paused momentarily as I approached the building but not enough to let passers-by know that I was a stranger to this site.

Despite my current state, and still red-eyed from weeping, I was still trying to uphold the persona that all was well with my world.

I approached the doors, gripped the handle, took a deep breath and pulled to enter. The doors were locked!

I tried an alternative door.

Locked!

I tried all the doors!

Locked!

Huh!

Feeling a little silly, as if I was being watched, I stood back, confused. I walked around the side of the building hoping to find a side or back door which was unlocked. Nothing!

I was bewildered.

It seemed that the church was CLOSED!

Remember, I grew up in a catholic church. It was always open - even when nothing was going on. You could always go in and sit peacefully, light a candle, kneel at the altar, pray, cry, read, even go to confession and leave feeling 'washed'!

This situation was baffling me.

I even felt embarrassed. I didn't like not knowing.

I tried the front doors again.

Same.

As I stepped back and lifted my eyes, I saw a notice board. In plain sight. With both my head and my eyes lowered, I hadn't noticed it.

It read, 'Service times, Sundays, 9.30am, 11.15am, 6.30pm'.

Really?

Here I was on Saturday afternoon, and this sign was telling me that this church wasn't 'open' at all today.

Surely not!

What was I to do until tomorrow?

I walked away.

Head down.

I went home.

I sat - and I cried.

All evening.

That night I slept an exhausted sleep.

I awoke in a daze.

Despite sleeping through the night, I still felt tired.

My eyes were sore.

My head hurt.

I was thirsty.

I did my best to get myself together, but I didn't feel good about myself. My eyes had become swollen from all the crying.

I wrapped up to protect myself from the cold and stepped outside.

The cold hit me full in the face (everywhere else was covered). It was a freezing February morning and although it was bright and crisp, I didn't appreciate it. The cold just added to the prolonged feeling of misery I had been feeling all weekend.

I persevered.

I caught the bus, as I had the day before, but this time a part of me wanted to turn back. I had calculated that, if the church was only open at set times, people were going to be there en-mass at those set times, therefore I was going to be surrounded by other people - in this state!

Approaching from a distance I could already see that today was going to be a very different scenario to yesterday. There was a crowd of people OUTSIDE of the church and more of them were pouring out of the doors as I approached.

They were chattering and laughing, greeting each other warmly and hugging! I was hesitant, but I pushed forward - I had come this far.

As I stood on the pavement outside the church, about to enter the building, I looked ahead - Sam!

I fled!

Speed walking around the building and toward the car parks!

I didn`t look back.

My head down, I circled the block and got on the next bus home!

I couldn't do it!

I had panicked.

As I shut my front door behind me I leaned against it again as I had done on that Friday evening - and this time I stayed there.

My mind was racing. All the way home I had focused on not being seen and not drawing attention to myself but now, in the safety of my own home, I felt a fool.

Eventually I rationalised that my reaction to seeing Sam, standing at the entrance of the church with his back to me, chatting to others were my erratic thoughts getting out of control.

I had summarised, in that split second, that if Sam saw me there he would think I was there to see him and that maybe I wanted more than just a friendship.

Whilst that wasn't the case at all, my mind had fed me that information and I had believed it - and reacted to it.

Now, here I was, right back where I started.

Needless to say, the tears came again - and now I was in a heap on the floor.

The thought of facing tomorrow loomed over me. The advance planner in me had kicked in. Going to work, looking like this, feeling like this - the risk of breaking down and crying at work - I couldn't, I just couldn't.

I had to do something.

I'm a fighter - but I had no fight left.

I had friends and family that I could call – my sister would have been there in a heartbeat - but I didn't want them at this moment.

I was yearning for something, for change, for direction - I didn't want sympathy or a shoulder to cry on - I'd done enough of that.

My thoughts were making me feel a bit angry.

Angry at myself for running away.

Angry for not knowing what to do right now.

I sat up from my curled-up position on the floor. I was tired and achy.

'Get up!' I told myself.

Come on.

Think.

I looked at the wall opposite and tried to put some thoughts together.

It came to me.

If Sam was there this morning, would he be there again this evening?

In the back of my mind, I remembered him telling me about a rota that all the singers and musicians had, to cover each of the services. I had suggested catching a movie once on a Sunday evening and he couldn't go because he was 'rota'd to play' that evening.

Earlier, when I saw him at the church entrance, he had had his bass with him!

That meant........he was unlikely to be at the evening service!

As I approached the entrance this time I walked slower and with less confidence.

This was now my third attempt to attend a church service in this building and I was feeling very foolish and very apprehensive.

I hesitated and scanned the entrance looking for Sam. I couldn't see him. I stepped forward.

A lovely looking elderly man, sharply dressed and standing just inside the door, greeted me and shook my hand.

I remember my hand feeling bigger than his. He was a small framed man with white hair and a uniquely shaped goatee.

`Good evening love` he said, making eye contact.

He looked happy.

I smiled at him and managed to respond.

As I stepped further in to the building I felt warmth - not the actual room temperature - a kind of inner warmth, like a hug from someone much larger than me.

I continued in and veered to the left.

This felt comfortable, homely.

It was an old building, 1960's, I thought, with lots of wood panelling. There was carpet on the floor and above me was a low ceiling – with fans. Ahead was a stage.

Despite lots of noise and movement from people chattering and children playing, it was…...nice!

I didn't know where to go or what to do but I tried not to make that obvious. This was so different from `church` that I knew. This was loud and active not sombre and quiet.

But I liked it.

I made my way to the back row on the far left and sat right against the brick exposed wall. There was a wooden wall behind me, so I felt hidden away from view.

I wanted this – to be hidden.

I sat with my head down and leaned into the wall as though it supported me.

I felt self-conscious, like I didn't fit. It was all alien to me and I was unsure of what to do, so I just sat.

People started to fill up the chairs, mostly at the front. They walked intentionally to their seats as if they had sat in them before - like children entering a classroom.

Familiar.

I observed them.

They took off their coats and hung them on the back of the chair in front.

I kept my coat on.

I wasn't cold.

I had expected to be, but I wasn't, not at all.

But I kept my coat on.

I always did.

My black coat was like a security blanket for me - a shield, if you like. It wasn't really suitable for this weather - it was more of an autumn coat, a mac. But I had many layers on underneath, so it did the job.

As more people filled the seats, I had a sense that something was about to happen.

I was startled as a loud noise filled the room. I can only describe it as a concert kicking off and the audience responding with claps and little `whoops` and cheers.

Everyone stood to their feet, almost in unison, and started to `two-step` to the beat.

I stood too, more as an act of obedience - but I didn't dance or clap – I felt too self-conscious.

Although the atmosphere felt......nice, I wasn't feeling joyful. I certainly didn't feel like dancing!

There were drums and guitars playing, keyboards and even bongos!

And then, singing!

Everyone was singing, like one enormous choir!

The words to the songs appeared on a huge screen over on the far right but no-one seemed to be looking at the words. They all seemed to know the words! Some had their eyes closed and their hands raised, others danced and clapped......I had never experienced anything like this!

I liked it.

The singing went on for quite a while, but it didn't seem too long for me. However, I was emotional. I became tearful again. And self-aware. Although no-one was looking at me - not that I could notice - I tried to keep it together, but it was difficult.

The music was so moving, the words so meaningful, I tried to sing along but mostly I closed my eyes and listened to the words being sung to me.

Each time I opened my eyes, tears flooded down my cheeks onto my coat. I'd wipe them and close my eyes again to stop more tears from falling but they just kept coming.

I felt weak.

I was relieved when everyone sat down. My legs couldn't have stood for much longer.

I was curious as to what would happen next.

There were some announcements and a collection and then the man at the front asked us to open our bibles.

I didn't have one.

Someone next to me held her bible open between us and I leaned in to show I appreciated the gesture.

She knew where to turn to when directed from the front - I knew none of this. I had a bible somewhere at home that I'd been given whilst at school, but I had not read it.

The leader began to talk, and everyone listened attentively. Some even made notes.

This was like an inspirational training session - not church as I knew it. As he continued speaking I found myself drinking in what he was saying and wondering how he knew so much about me! My tears had dried up now and I was intrigued and captured by every word he spoke.

Did this man know me?

"And as I close".

It was coming to an end. The talk was about to finish.

What now?

Everyone closed their eyes and dropped their heads as though praying but the man was still speaking. He was asking if anyone wanted to have a relationship with Jesus and have their life transformed. He spoke about a new direction and having purpose.

My hand was up in the air! I didn't consciously make the decision to put it up, but there it was. And in the next minute I was walking towards this man, eagerly, as though he was going to give me something that would solve all my problems. A cure! A remedy! A prescription! At the very least, some instructions.

I stood there at the front of the church, with others, waiting.

Expecting.

He prayed, and I repeated the prayer.

Someone came to me and gave me something to read and a small bible. They said, `Welcome`.

I took what I was given and returned to my seat to get my bag.

People were leaving now.

I followed them out.

Head down.

Baffled.

Changed.

3 PLANTED

From that point on I was transformed. I fell in love for the very first time.

Whilst nothing much changed outwardly, on the inside I was unrecognisable. I began to live my life as though I had much to look forward to.

Most of my time was spent at the church.

As well as the services on a Sunday, of which I would go to at least two of the services, morning and evening - I would also attend other meetings that took place throughout the week. I would offer to do whatever needed doing and was really enjoying the sense of belonging that it brought.

As I spent more and more time at the church I made friends with people of all ages.

Ilford Elim had become my home.

Some things were still difficult - money was tight for instance and I still struggled with self-awareness but on the whole life became much more positive. I no longer felt lonely as I spent my time productively and I took time to get to know my new-found love - Jesus!

As time passed, I became more established within certain ministries and took on more responsibility. I joined the media team and the choir, and I would attend small groups and events. I was now 28 years old and felt more fulfilled than I ever had.

Life was good!

Love was good.

Genuine love from above.

It was so good!

So much was happening to me emotionally and mentally. I was being straightened out, if you like - cleansed from within.

As I continued to serve God and His church I gained more confidence in myself and my ability. I stepped out into areas I never would have before.

One day I felt the urge to talk to God about relationships.

I had avoided this before as it had always been a `messy` area for me - inconsistent, unfulfilling, short-lived and downright annoying if the truth be told. But as the years passed I was mindful that time was passing, and this was an area that I had `put aside`.

I began to pray regularly about this specific area of my life and I found myself entering another level of intimacy with God.

I was opening up and being more vulnerable with Him than I had ever been before, with anyone! I spoke honestly, holding nothing back.

At times I wept, other times I was angry. Not with God, but I would vent at Him.

Often, I stayed silent and listened for God's voice in the silence of my mind.

This area became very intimate between God and me.

I shared it with no-one.

After months and months of prayer God gave me these words, `Be a wife before you're a wife!` and led me to Isaiah 54:5;

'For your Maker is your husband, the Lord of hosts is His name; And your Redeemer is the Holy One of Israel; He is called the God of the whole earth.' NKJV

Honestly? I was devastated!

I interpreted this to mean I was to remain unmarried with no children and be devoted to God for the rest of my life!

I had attended a convent school in my younger days and the vision of the nuns that taught me flashed into my mind!

I didn't understand this.

I began to question God.

When I had first become a Christian, I had asked God to keep me away from any entanglements regarding relationships. I had asked Him to 'save' me for my husband. I didn't want to date guys in the church for it to come to nothing. I wanted to be presented with my husband at the right time so that I could invest in the relationship that would then lead to marriage, and so on.

Had I doomed myself?

Had God misunderstood?

Did I not make myself clear?

Did it not say in Psalms 37:4;

`Delight yourself also in the Lord, And He shall give you the desires of your heart.` NKJV

Was I not delighting myself in the Lord?

What did that even mean?

To say I was confused was an understatement.

And 'be a wife before you're a wife', what does THAT mean!?

I just didn't understand any of it.

As this was such an intimate area between myself and God I decided not to ask anyone what they thought it might mean. I went back to God and left it with Him.

I heard nothing back, but I did notice myself changing.

My attitude towards others was shifting.

I was becoming more generous, less critical, caring, sharing, open to new ideas. Basically, God was shifting me from single mode to 'double' mode - teaching me how to consider others in all that I did.

He taught me how to listen instead of just speaking.

How to appreciate other people's views and opinions.

It was subtle, but I felt the change.

In my home I changed too.

Previously, my home had been my private, safe-haven. I didn't invite people over or open my home to others. That had been my private space that very few people entered - including my family. I would spend time with others outside of my home and return to my safe place, finding it just how I left it.

But now, I felt the urge to host others.

Don't get me wrong, I wasn't completely transformed into the 'hostess with the mostest', but I would invite a friend over now and then, and it felt good.

One Sunday morning, following the 11.15am service, a dear auntie, whom God had placed in my life, came over to talk to me.

She told me that God had laid on her heart that she was to pray and fast with me regarding my help-mate. (I know that is not the biblically correct term for the husband, but that is what she said, and so, I am saying it to you verbatim).

I was stunned.

It was so out of the blue. We hadn't had a discussion about this and I hadn't shared with her what God had said to me about being a wife.

We hugged and agreed that we would pray and fast on the 20th of every month until my husband was `delivered`.

And so, we did.

We didn't get together to do this, we just prayed and fasted wherever we were on the 20th of each month, as agreed.

Three years passed.

Yes, three YEARS!

My thirtieth birthday came and went. In my mind, in my planning, my thirtieth birthday was symbolic of my future. To celebrate, I planned a black-tie dinner party in a private room in London. I invited my closest friends at the time and as I prepared the seating plan for the evening I left a vacant space beside my seat. That was for my future husband. I told myself, 'God will fill that space with the person He has chosen for me'.

That space stayed vacant.

I learned that night not to force the hand of God.

But God was hard at work.

He would often remind me that He hadn't forgotten me, either with a dream, a song, a word from someone but mostly through His word.

Deep down, in the quiet place of my soul, I knew I was to be a wife and mother - and I trusted my God to deliver.

Of course, there were moments, usually sunny Sunday afternoons when it seemed that everyone had someone to be with, that I questioned when my time would come, but generally I just pushed on doing my best to fulfil what God was calling me to do during any given season.

My best friend and I would hang out and talk about our future spouses and we'd pray that God's will would be fulfilled in both our lives. We were both at a similar stage, him desiring a wife, and me desiring a husband, and we knew without a doubt that God would do it. Actually, he was a step ahead of me.

We started to feel the call from God to distance ourselves from each other. We didn't always understand it but as we spent less and less time with each other I certainly questioned what God was 'up to'.

In truth, all my friends were gradually 'doing their own thing' and this upset me a little.

Actually, a lot!

They never seemed to be available anymore, never answered my calls. I began to wonder if I had caused them some offence, without realising.

In hindsight, it all made sense, but at the time it was really quite painful.

Christmas and New Year were fast approaching and a small group of us decided to go to Watford to spend New Year with a friend who lived there.

She had been invited to a party and invited us along.

We drove up to her place on New Year's Eve and arrived in a festive mood. Shortly after arriving at her place and settling in we unanimously agreed to not go to the party after all but to have a quiet New Year in with some nibbles and girly chat.

We lounged on the floor and just caught up with each other - we hadn't seen each other in a while.

Then came the suggestion, 'Why don't we do a list of what we'd like to see God do in our lives in the coming months and years?'

I was chosen to go first.

I thought about it briefly and spoke whatever came to my mind.

Someone was taking notes so that we could remember what had been said and refer back to those notes in time to come.

As I finished speaking, and as we were about to move on to the next person, I blurted, 'Oh, and I need to reconcile with my Dad!'

I have no idea where that came from, it was just there, and I spoke it.

And now it was written down.

Evidence.

As I was handed the piece of paper I stared at it and knitted my brows together, confused. I had never had this desire before. Yes, God had laid this on my heart a number of times over the last few years. I knew He was willing me to forgive my dad and I had told Him that I had. I was sure that I had. I had put it out of my mind as a done deed, I had ticked that box and moved on.

Or so, I thought.

What was this then?

Reconciliation?

If I wasn't mistaken, that would require making some kind of contact with him.

Surely not!

Was that really necessary?

Would that serve any purpose?

Would that add to me in any way?

I didn't even know where he was!

I put the piece of paper away.

We finished our lists and we prayed over them vowing to share testimonies when the desires we had listed came into play.

The rest of the evening was spent chattering, laughing, eating and celebrating the New Year when it eventually arrived.

It was a great night, really empowering and encouraging but a small part of my focus remained on what was written on my list.

Following that evening, I would think about what God had placed in my heart and I'd talk to Him about it. I would reason with Him about how it could play out. 'Maybe I could be walking down the street one day and he (my dad) would be walking the opposite way, toward me, and I'd say "Hi" and carry on walking.

Would that suffice?

I sensed that God was saying, 'Are you God, or am I? You can`t tell me how this is going to happen!'

So, I waited, not knowing how this would all materialize.

But as the days and weeks went by the urge to deal with this reconciliation got stronger and stronger. It just wouldn't leave me alone. It came to my mind constantly throughout each day. I knew it had to be dealt with, but I didn't know how. No matter how many pictures and scenarios I tried to build in my head of how I could reconcile with my dad nothing felt right.

Then it came to me.

I didn't like it, but it came to me, clear as anything.

Call him!

Pick up the phone and call him!

It was like a light had come on!

Literally!

Now, whilst this doesn't seem profound or revolutionary to most people, to me this was a breakthrough. An absolute leap forward from where I had been even 3 months prior.

Let me fill you in.

As previously mentioned, my parents divorced when I was very young.

My sister and I would visit our dad on Sundays.

Every Sunday.

For years!

My sister is three and a half years older than me which meant that when she reached a certain age she decided she no longer wanted to visit him each Sunday, so she stopped.

Just like that.

This left me to visit alone.

It was ok. I'd arrive at lunchtime and watch the Eastenders omnibus on TV. Then I'd do my homework and practice my guitar and it was time to go home.

My dad would always pick us up and drop us home, but he never came near the house where we had grown up and still lived. He'd park a few houses down and we'd walk up to meet him.

When my sister stopped coming I would walk those few yards alone.

We didn't speak much in the car, my dad and me.

We didn't speak much at his house either. When my sister still visited with me we would play outside together, running up the grassy hill and rolling down it again. Or, swinging as high as we could on the swings, singing,

"FAME! I'm gonna live forever! I'm gonna learn how to fly, HIGH!"

Good times.

Great times actually.

But once she stopped coming to visit that all ended.

I would stay in the flat and pass the time on my own. Dad would sit in the room with me, but we didn't say much.

At the age of thirteen, following a visit to the Caribbean with my mum, I went to visit my dad as usual on the following Sunday.

My brother took me there that day, I can't recall why, but when we arrived dad was in the bath, so my brother left, and I settled down to watch Eastenders, as usual.

The next thing I recall was my dad standing over me, (I was sitting in an armchair), saying that I hadn't even sent him as much as a postcard and that he was taking me home.

I was dumbstruck.

Out of respect for my dad I didn't ask any questions or protest in any way - but I wanted to.

I hadn't sent anyone a postcard.

This seemed like a big fuss over nothing, but I didn't dare state this.

Silently, I gathered my things and walked to the car not daring to even look at him.

He seemed so angry.

The ride home was silent and unfamiliar. We were usually silent, but I wasn't accustomed to making this return journey so early in the day.

As we arrived at the corner of the street where our usual farewell exchange took place, I didn't know then that it would be the last time we would do this.

As I released my seatbelt and leaned forward to collect my bag from the foot well in front of me, he uttered the words that would stay with me for many years to come,

"I'll see you when I see you, and if anyone asks you who your dad is, say you haven't got one."

And he was gone.

4 BUILDING BRIDGES

Seventeen years on, grasping the phone, heart pounding, I dialled the number. It didn't ring long enough. I didn't have time to change my mind again.

"Hello?"

He sounded the same.

I paused.

I hadn`t rehearsed what to say.

"Hello Dad?" I said, as though it was a question.

Silence.

Maybe three seconds pause, but it seemed so much longer as both of us had no idea what was about to happen.

He said my name. This was completely out of the blue for him and, for a moment, I wondered what that must have felt like.

I imagined him sitting forward in his armchair, the one where I used to sit.

My sister had advised me, when she gave me his number that he still lived in the same flat where we used to visit him all those years ago.

"Yes, hello dad."

I was smiling. I was not even sure why, but the smile was there and as I fidgeted with the belt of my dressing gown I felt small again. Like a child.

But it didn't last.

"What do you want?" he asked, his voice quickly evolving from intrigue to defence.

"Err......I don't want anything. I just......"

He cut in mid-sentence, "Are you sick? Do you need money?"

I tried to empathize with his line of questioning and place myself in his shoes, but no, this was getting too much.

The rejection was happening all over again.

I started to recoil.

I wanted to slam the phone down and respectfully but firmly shout at God telling him I had tried but, look......!

In that split-second God jumped in.

He reminded me that I had a relationship with Him and therefore had had an opportunity to receive forgiveness and love. I had been shown patience, understanding and grace and had been given time to heal and repair.

My dad had not had any of this and would not understand this act of reconciliation.

I had to be the bigger person.

I had to persevere.

The next words I spoke were the hardest I'd ever spoken but the most liberating and life changing.

"Dad, I don't want anything from you. I just think it's time we put the past behind us and try to build something from this day forward."

Whilst these words were not profound in any way, they were life changing - for both my dad and me. For, at that moment, the child disappeared, and I spoke with my dad adult to adult.

We continued to speak. For two hours actually - and by the end of the conversation the child returned, and my dad was telling me he loved me and wanted to see me.

It wasn't all idyllic, don't get me wrong.

There were moments where he would say something that would make me pull the phone away from my ear, hold it in front of me and roll my eyes or express disbelief - like when he told me he forgave me - for WHAT!

I let it go.

It wasn't worth getting into.

But, in general, it was mind-blowing to think that; I was here, talking to my dad.

I NEVER thought that would happen. I had had so much hatred and bitterness towards him for rejecting me and it had reflected in my relationships.

I wouldn't allow anyone to get close to me. Close to my heart.

If my own father could reject and disown me why wouldn't every other man in my life do the same – or worse!

I had never vocalised those 'three words' to any man and I'd vowed I never would. My thinking was, if I tell him I love him, I would be giving him the power to hurt me – to break me.

So now, my dad is telling me he loves me on the other end of the phone.......and I'm saying it back!

WHAT ON EARTH?

And yet, I was still to hear the words that would completely melt any ice that was still left in my heart.

"What do you look like?"

I dropped my head back against my headboard and tears welled up in my eyes.

Despite what he had done to me, and the years of bondage I had been in because of him, I resolved, in that moment, that no parent should ever have to ask that question of their child.

Whoever was at fault, no matter the circumstances, that just didn't sit right with me.

I couldn't answer the question.

What could I say?

I didn't know whether I looked like him. I couldn't really remember what he looked like. I had no pictures of him. None of us did.

I realised, in that moment, that *I* wanted to see him.

Without me saying it, he confirmed that he was thinking the same thing - he promptly asked if he could see me.

We arranged for me to visit him the next day and we ended the call.

I sat in my bed, a flurry of feelings pounding through my body.

I stared at the phone in my hand and just sat in silence recalling the conversation that had taken place.

I burst out laughing.

Despite my nerves and apprehension about making the call I was so delighted that I had.

As a whole, it had gone better than I could ever have imagined - despite the shaky start.

I exhaled and uttered the words, "Thank you Lord", and my mind quickly fast forwarded to the next day when I would meet my dad for the first time in seventeen years.

As I stepped off the DLR and made my way to his flat, it all came flooding back.

It all looked the same - mostly.

Some things had been added or upgraded - like signage or railings but on the whole, it seemed like I'd only been gone a short while.

But I hadn't.

It had been an incredibly long time and a lot had changed. In my life anyway.

I approached the front door – it looked the same. It *felt* the same. Like stepping back in time.

I wanted to pause longer but I wondered whether he could see me through the curtains that hung in the window.

He was expecting me - was he looking out for me?

I rang the doorbell and the door opened almost instantly.

The man I saw was immediately recognisable but so different to what I expected? I hadn't known what to expect. I had very little memory of him. Despite being thirteen when I last saw him, my mind and emotions had blocked all imagery of him out - to protect me, I'm sure.

He was small. Shorter than me, and his hair was white. It was a full head of wavy hair, freshly cut and shaped, but white all over.

As he said my name, with a smile on his face and disbelief in his eyes he reached out and took my arm to gently pull me inside.

It was like stepping into a museum of his life.

The dark hallway was just as I remembered it.

It felt very warm, just as it always had before. The coat hooks on the left and the mirror at the end, just before you entered the kitchen, were all reminders of my Sundays spent here as a child.

Although he had obviously decorated over the years, the colour scheme, furniture and overall decor was the same style as it had been back then.

As I turned and entered the lounge the large windows with perfectly hung, ceiling to floor curtains stirred my memory once again. I slowed my steps as I observed a gallery of photographs on his large, wooden sideboard, situated to my right, against the wall. I drew closer.

Displays of photographs, in anyone's home, always told me so much about the person that lived there. Part of me wanted to look, but another part of me didn't want to be reminded that I wasn't a part of this household – a part of this history.

But I was curious.

What I did want to know was – who was this man?

Yes, he was my father. But I didn't know him.

Although he had rejected me at thirteen, I had not lived with him from the age of five. And, even then, we did not have a close relationship with him, even when he was living at home with us. He was the disciplinarian. He stated the rules and we did our best to live by them. As young children we often failed to abide by those rules.

And we paid the price. We lived in fear of him – tension was ever-present in our home.

As I stepped closer and stooped to observe the display, I was taken aback.

Many of the photographs were of my sister and I, as children.

This caught me off guard. I really wasn't expecting to see what I saw.

I felt....... guilty!

In my mind, he had forgotten all about us and had moved on with his life, choosing to leave us out of it. Had I been wrong all this time?

I told myself it didn't matter - we were going to focus on the future, not the past.

He left my side and disappeared momentarily into the kitchen. I watched him go. He walked with a slight limp.

I was still standing with my coat on gazing at the pictures – not really seeing them but looking at the pictures, or maybe the movies, that were playing in my mind's eye, when he returned and handed me a worn, tarnished bowl. It was yellow in colour, plastic. The type a child would eat breakfast cereal from.

It struck me.

I remembered.

It had been *my* cereal bowl, when I was a baby.

He had kept it! All this time! Not in a loft or garage. In his kitchen! It would now be almost thirty years old!

He had moved so many times before settling in this flat, and he hadn't lost or misplaced it. He hadn't thrown it away.

Any ounce of anger or bitterness I had left disappeared in that moment.

As I turned the bowl around and around in my hands, I..........

I shut down my thoughts.

I couldn't deal with them all. They were coming at me at a rate that was too much to cope with in this moment, in this place.

I literally froze them.

I went into my safe mode – autopilot.

I knew I would unpack those feelings again – maybe later. In the safety of my own home. In private. But not now. I couldn't do this now.

I couldn't tell you what we talked about during that visit. It didn't matter.

I had no questions about the past.

I didn't want to go there.

I wanted to move forward, and that's what we did.

I sat with him, my dad, for just over an hour before I left, promising to visit again soon.

As I walked away, my dad watched me until I reached the end of the long path.

I turned back to wave, just before I was out of view. He waved back, and this was to become our little ritual in the years to come.

He would always wait and watch, and I would always wave.

Our 'thing'.

As I continued walking, now out of sight, a familiar voice said, "I now release you into your marriage!"

I knew that voice, but today, in that moment, it seemed louder and clearer than ever before. I felt sure that, if someone had been with me they would have heard it too.

I had obeyed.

I had believed.

I was about to receive….my blessing!

5 NEW BEGINNINGS

By obeying God and making that call to my father, I encountered the biggest breakthrough I had had in my walk with God.

The biggest breakthrough ever, if I'm honest!

Things really took a turn after that. As far as I was concerned, I had climbed the highest mountain and swam the deepest sea and I was ready to do whatever God asked of me.

I trusted Him now.

He had proven Himself to me and despite the fear I had felt I could now see that the very thing that I thought would cause me pain and rejection all over again had actually brought healing and restoration.

I hadn't realised, until that point, as I walked away from my father's home, that I had lived such a suppressed, imprisoned life.

Despite others telling me that my father's rejection was having an effect on my life, I hadn't believed them.

Not only had I not believed them, I wasn't even listening to them. I didn't want to hear it.

As far as I was concerned, they knew nothing about me and didn't have the right to speak about my life or my family.

I would nod politely and excuse myself or just zone out when they were speaking.

Now, in hindsight, I could understand what they had all been trying to express to me.

The sense of release and freedom was tangible.

I walked without fear.

Fear of bumping into him.

Fear of someone asking me about him.

Fear of having to explain why I have no contact with him, etc, etc.

I had learnt, through becoming a Christian that I was to honour my mother and father. It was also explained to me that I was to honour them whether they deserved it or not. So, the way I had spoken about my father in the past (on the odd occasion that I had) was no longer acceptable. My mindset had been changed, and so, what I spoke also changed.

This, in turn, changed my heart.

With all this change going on I was beginning to see a new me materialising.

I no longer denied that I wanted a husband – either to myself or to others.

There was a time when, if others mentioned the word 'husband' I would recoil and enforce the fact that I was not looking for a husband and did not NEED to have someone in my life!

That I was 'just *fine*' as I was and that, 'when the time came.... then great.... but...until then...I was just *fine.*'

I'm not sure whether I was convincing them or myself but, it was time to let all of that go.

As my praying and fasting continued, the preparations continued.

And so did the trials!

One by one, the offers came.

Now please, hear my heart as I explain this next part.

In no way am I saying that men were falling at my feet!

Not at all – quite the opposite.

But there were a few 'suitors' that made themselves *known*, shall we say?

I won't add too much detail, as they may be identifiable, but I'll give you a snippet of the deception that I encountered along the way.

Whilst I was still 'finding my way' as a Christian and trying to learn and understand God's word and the teachings from Sunday services etc, I met (let's call him) Mike.

Mike came and introduced himself to me after a service and we got talking. I was not attracted to Mike in any way, but he was friendly, so we spoke after services and meetings and then went our separate ways.

One day Mike asked me where I lived. I told him the area – he lived in the same area.

What quickly unfolded was Mike wanted to walk me home.

The walks home developed into cups of tea whilst we studied the bible.

I'll give Mike the credit he deserves, he did help me to understand my scriptures better, but Mike wasn't prepared to keep it at that.

One day whilst walking 'home' together he slipped his hand into mine.

I ripped my hand away and asked him what he was doing.

Mike tried to explain and apologised for overstepping the mark.

Believing that he had got the message loud and clear, that I was not interested in him in that way, we carried on with our study sessions.

One evening, whilst at my place, Mike tells me he 'can't be bothered to go home' (a 15-minute walk away) and decides that he is going across the road to the shop to buy a toothbrush and will 'crash on my sofa'.

Let's just say, that was the end of that!

Mike was history.

We greeted each other in church but that was it.

I watched from a distance over the following weeks whilst he prepped his next victim.

Carl was a bit older than me.

I didn't know how much older, but he was definitely a good 8-10 years my senior, or so he seemed.

One Sunday morning, at the end of the service, I had gone to the front for prayer and was very, *very* emotional.

I was sobbing as I returned to my seat. My face was a mess and I knew it.

I started to gather my things to head for the ladies' toilet and there was Carl.

Standing too close for comfort and *appearing* very concerned about my *state*.

Everything in me wanted to side-step him and disappear from his presence, but he was determined. He kept blocking my way.

He said something along the lines of, "I've been wanting to speak to you for a while, but you always seem to disappear after the service."

Still conscious of my dreadful state, I thought, 'Err, I'd like to disappear right now if you wouldn't mind'.

But I said nothing.

I couldn't.

It would have been a messy blubber.

I kept quiet and kept my eyes down.

Carl continued to show concern, but I didn't want it.

I wanted to go.

He kept asking if I was okay.

I lied, nodding that I was. But I was getting irritated.

After a couple of minutes of this Carl asked if he could meet with me to discuss something.

I didn't respond straight away. I didn't know what he was talking about.

I didn't care.

I just wanted to sort myself out.

He kept talking about meeting up and suggested meeting later that week.

With frustration setting in I agreed to meet him as a way of escaping the scene.

I walked away and bolted to the ladies not even thinking about what just happened.

A few evenings later I walked into the wine bar where we had agreed to meet and there was Carl.

Seeing him outside of the church setting felt odd.

He was dressed more casually, as was I, but something felt odd.

He had a look on his face that was making me knit my eyebrows together in wonder.

He greeted me with a kiss on each cheek.

Too close - again.

Too familiar.

He held my upper arms and squeezed as he planted those kisses.

I didn't like it.

I should have made my excuses right there and then and fled the scene, but manners and etiquette got the better of me. I remained at the scene.

We ordered drinks and the 'interview' began.

He did – he actually interviewed me. He just fired questions at me as though I was applying for the prestigious role of wife and mother to his children.

Defiance kicked in quickly and I asked him what he was doing.

I reminded him that he had asked to meet so that he could talk to me about something.

He smiled, knowingly, as though he had won.

His deception had got me here and now he was weaving his web. When he saw that his line of questioning was getting him nowhere he changed direction.

He asked me, "So, do you like my physique?"

I nearly spat my drink out!

"Pardon?" I asked.

I didn't really want him to repeat the question, but I really didn't know what else to say in that moment. My question wasn't really a question. It was more of an expression, but he chose to answer it anyway.

He repeated, "Do you like my physique?" Now, he was thrusting his chest forward as if to give me a better view.

He continued quickly by enlightening me on how many times he went to the gym and that he could get me a visitor pass if I wanted to come with him.

I politely declined and tuned out of the nonsense.

Now, all I could think about was how to escape this awful situation, and I was berating myself for getting into it in the first place.

But Carl, well.... he was on a roll.

Do you know what he said next?

I'll tell you.

The words are etched in my mind forever.

"Do you know, Sonia, if you were fat, dark-skinned or had children you would not be sitting here with me now".

I kid you not!

Those were his *exact* words.

I'll never forget them.

For the first and only time in my whole life I wanted to go to the ladies' bathroom and climb out of a window and escape, like they did in the movies.

My only hesitation was that I was likely to see Carl at church that Sunday and I just didn't want to have to deal with unfinished business. So, instead, I stood up, excused myself and left the bar.

As I walked to the underground station, fast, I couldn't resist calling my sister and telling her about the madness I had just experienced.

She cried with laughter and asked me to repeat what he had said numerous times, just so the hysterics could continue.

Thanks to her I was able to laugh about it too at that point.

But it wasn't over.

Carl sent me a message asking if we could meet again as 'he had enjoyed our time together!'

My sister insisted that I meet him to tell him that we could not see each other again.

I was happy to reply with a text message and end it there, but she was insistent that I *do things properly*.

So, reluctantly, I met Carl again and made it clear that his comments and suggestions had been inappropriate and unwelcome (especially as he wasn't slim, *and* he had a child).

I tried to make him understand that saying these things were not acceptable and were rather off-putting to say the least.

I don't think he got it, but my job was done. Carl was history.

Whilst employed as a conference manager at a hotel, Andrew came to my place of work wanting to hire a space for his church to use for their meetings.

He was suited and professional and as we sat down to go through the details of his requirements we spoke very easily with no pauses or silences.

As we neared the end of the meeting, Andrew asked about my plans for the future with regards to career.

I wasn't offended by this as Andrew was a business advisor by profession and his speciality was helping people start up in business.

We started to talk about business plans etc and he was very helpful in directing me in what I needed to do to get my business idea off the ground.

As I had another appointment coming in to see me I advised that I'd have to wrap up our meeting.

Andrew suggested that we meet another time to discuss my business plans further.

I was happy to do this, and we agreed to meet at a local restaurant.

I brought along all my paperwork and met Andrew at the suggested location.

As we sat down I began to start up the conversation where we had left off.

Andrew 'entertained' my line of conversation for a while and listened to me speak, and then he asked,

"So, do you have any brothers or sisters?"

My immediate thought was, 'What does that have to do with my business plan?'

My secondary thought was, 'Here we go again!'

Andrew was a nice enough guy, but I just wasn't looking for that right now. I didn't want to get into a relationship at that point. I just wanted to be with God and grow in Him.

Let me add, these 'episodes' with Mike, Carl and Andrew all took place long before my reconciliation with my dad and so I was in a very different place and not at all thinking about relationships.

To summarise the Andrew situation – it ended with him banging on my front door one day telling me he was unable to sleep, and that God had revealed to him that I was to be his wife.

By that point, the sheer sight of him irritated me and I didn't even like being in his presence.

How on earth would the loving, caring, fatherly God that I serve give me a husband I didn't even like being around.

That made absolutely no sense to me.

Andrew was history.

My final example was a guy who was a member of my church and had started attending just one year after I given my life to Christ.

We hadn't spoken to each other and moved in different circles, but I knew of him.

At our annual Church Weekend Away, which was attended by over 200 people, he had been serving with the youth ministry in a different part of the enormous, historical building and so I hadn't really seen him throughout the weekend.

But on the Saturday evening, following the entertainment session, I was sat with a group of female friends, just talking and laughing – as you do.

I looked up and saw Rob standing at the door, looking in to the room to see what was happening. He looked in my direction and so I beckoned him over (I have no idea why). As he approached I said to him, "I need to find you a wife!"

I have absolutely no idea why I said it, but he laughed and sat down next to me.

I began to point out potential matches for him.

He just laughed it off.

I realised I must have been embarrassing him and changed the subject to his mum who had passed away just earlier that month. As I said, I hadn't spoken with Rob before this point, but I had heard from other church members that his mum had passed away.

He began to respond, but I jumped in, apologising for raising a subject that was so sensitive. He corrected me and told me it was quite the opposite.

He explained that he wanted to talk about his mum, but everybody seemed to be avoiding the subject of his mum's death because they assumed it was too painful for him to talk about at this stage.

So, we talked.

And talked

And talked.

The room we were in had cleared, as people made their way to bed or other rooms - but we hadn't noticed.

The following morning, as I entered the breakfast room Rob beckoned me over to where he was sitting.

I sat with him and again the room cleared as everyone finished eating but we were oblivious to it all.

Eventually, we parted ways and left for home. It was a Sunday.

The following Sunday, back at our own church now, the 11.15am service had started, and I was worshipping at the front of the church.

Midway into the second song, the usher parted me and the person next to me and placed Rob right there!

I noticed his smell first.... he smelt good! Really good.

As he joined in the worship, I could hear him singing.... he could sing!

Then, as we sat to hear the notices, I was noticing his hands. Nice hands, slender but not feminine.

What was this?

I was starting to get feelings, for him!

I had been single for five years.

This felt strange and a little uncomfortable.

By now, I had reconciled with my Dad and God had told me that I was released into my marriage.

God had also sent that auntie in the church to pray and fast with me regarding a helpmate. We had done that, faithfully, for the last three years.

I believed that God would give me a husband as that was the desire of my heart, but it always felt as though it was around the corner.

Now, don't get me wrong, at that point, as I took in the scent and the sound of Rob and stared at his hands as they turned the pages of his bible, I wasn't thinking, 'Is this my husband?'

I just knew I was experiencing some feelings I hadn't felt in a long time, if ever.

I tried to focus on the rest of the teaching, but I'll be honest, I couldn't.

After the service, Rob turned and talked to me and we flowed easily in conversation.

He was on the committee of a social ministry that organised events for our church and he had a big New Year event coming up.

At the time, I was in event management as a profession, so we talked about ideas and concepts that would make his event a success.

It was obvious that neither of us wanted to part ways, but we did, and we agreed to both attend the evening service later that day.

Following the evening service, as we left the building, Rob asked where I had parked my car. We were in different car parks.

He suggested that he walk me to my car, and then I drive him round to his. I was happy to do this.

As we got into my car and I turned on the engine, familiar music flooded the car.

Freddie McGregor was singing, '*Push comes to shove*' and Rob asks me, "What do you know about these tunes?"

I replied with, "I was listening to these tunes before you were born!"

We continued to banter as I drove, and his car was in sight - far too soon. I liked being with him and our time together kept being cut short.

We had exchanged mobile numbers to communicate about the upcoming event but that evening we communicated about songs from back-in-the-day, people we knew, food we liked etc.

The event wasn't even mentioned.

The following day the banter turned to flirtation as we continued our communication via

email. I didn't get much work done, if I'm honest –
I was in a different place.

6 ON BOARD

A week later, and following continuous communication via text and email, Rob and I were due to serve the youth ministry at a special Christmas event they had organised. We had both agreed to do this long before we had started talking at the Church Weekend Away and Rob was particularly excited that we were both going to be there.

Don't get me wrong – I also wanted to spend time with Rob but after all our constant communication throughout the week, not to mention all the other things I had going on at that time, I was exhausted. I was at the point of pulling out (which was quite unlike me) but I really was shattered.

But Rob said the magic words that had me getting dressed and ready to leave at lightning speed. He said, 'You have to come. I want to see you.'

Now, you may be thinking that those words were not particularly dynamic in any way but let me enlighten you to my thoughts and feelings at the time.

In *five years,* in fact, in reality, it was much, much, *much* longer than that, I had not had someone express that they wanted to spend time with me. Just me. Not in that way. Friends and family, yes. But hearing Rob say that just triggered something within me.

He *wanted to spend time with me.*

He *wanted to see me.*

Me.

I was becoming special to someone.

Rob was providing security at the entrance on the ground floor of the venue whilst I was helping to serve the food up on the 1st floor. The kitchen, however, was on the ground floor and I had to pass the entrance each time I went back and forth to the kitchen.

Each time I passed the entrance I stole a glance at Rob as he masterfully managed the security. I don't mind adding that I had a little strut in my step and an extra sway in my hips each time I passed by. My feet were killing me, but my heeled boots looked better than flats, so I bore the pain.

A soldier for the cause!

My duties were over long before Rob's – he had to stay until the end, but there I was - like a groupie, hanging about by the door talking to Rob whilst he fulfilled his commitment.

As the evening ended Rob advised me that he was going to get his hair cut and would call me afterward.

By then, I was even more tired than I had been before, and I was looking forward to getting some sleep. But Rob insisted that he needed to speak to me and so I relented.

I knew by that point that things were developing between us and we needed to address the elephant in the room!

Despite being able to speak so easily over the previous couple of weeks, when the phone rang a couple of hours later, I felt nervous.

This was the point where we were to clarify where this was going.

I began to speak but I found myself stuttering and searching for words that wouldn't come. Yes, I was super tired, but I don't think that was the real reason.

Rob took the reins.

He was masterful and sure, but not dominating.

He informed me that he liked me, and he felt I liked him too.

I didn't say anything......but I silently agreed.

He suggested we move forward as a couple and continue to seek God as we journeyed together.

Honestly, I was scared.

This was big.

I know I'd prayed for this – prayed and fasted! For three years!

But suddenly it was here, and it was.... BIG!!

Whilst many would be delighted to have met the person that could potentially become their life partner, I was incredibly nervous.

Not only did I want to be sure that this was of God, but I was also unsure of Christian relationships and what they looked like.

Previously, prior to becoming a Christian, I had walked away from relationships very easily. I did not attach myself to anyone and certainly didn't invest in long term commitments because I felt sure they would turn sour and eventually end.

Let me tell you why.

From a very young age I saw dishonesty and infidelity displayed in my home and my surroundings.

I witnessed these things on a daily basis and didn't see any examples of true commitment and loyalty.

Oh, I saw loyalty, but mixed with pain and hurt.

As I grew older, and started dating, I experienced this same behaviour in my own relationships.

I saw men as being fickle and disloyal.

I learnt to be distant, cold and guarded.

I watched my own mother operate as a single parent, putting our needs before her own whilst simultaneously holding her head high.

She became my role model.

I saw her strength and resilience and I admired the way she orchestrated her life to fit around her children so that we never felt unloved or in need.

My mother, the eldest female of thirteen children, didn't have the opportunity or exposure to education that her siblings had as she was required to assist with their upbringing. Much of this I didn't know at that early stage but what I did know was I could rely on her.

She was there.

She committed, she loved, she worked hard, she had standards and she set boundaries.

I saw all of this displayed by a woman – the head of our home.

I did not see this in a man.

Any man.

There were no examples for me.

Many of my friend's homes were the same. Those who had fathers present (very few) were not physically present at all.

I now understand that they were working or resting at the times that I would be in their homes, but my point is, I didn't SEE examples of how men added or contributed to their family.

Now, the example I saw in my mother began to mould my character.

I liked her strength.

I loved the way she got things done.

I loved that no obstacle stood in her way.

I mostly admired the fact that she would somehow operate beyond the status quo.

She found a way to make things work.

When employment dictated that she would not be home to see us off to school or collect us from school, she found another way. Rather than do one full time job to put food on our table and clothes on our backs, she would do three part time jobs which meant she could be there at the relevant times so that we did not experience her continued absence.

It was sacrificial and exhausting, but she recognised that it was for a season – she taught me that.

I saw resilience in her.

I also saw determination.

However, as I developed, this strength and resilience became my trademark and I became fiercely independent, declaring that I needed no-one else to exist.

I relied on no-one, and, coupled with my rejection from my father, I became quite a force to be reckoned with.

At sixteen I gained employment in a bank in central London and my income was sufficient to support my own independence.

Driving and purchasing my first car at eighteen offered me a new form of freedom.

Into my twenties this independence was reinforced as I changed careers and went into event management.

I began travelling and working in prestigious establishments – I got a taste of a different life. The world was offering me much of what I hadn't had growing up.

First class and five stars had become the standard for me at that stage.

I would date, but it was always short-lived.
I didn't invest in relationships.
I didn't allow anyone in.
I felt very much in control.
Until things began to spiral out of control.

Relationships didn't last, as I didn't know how to sustain them.

Money was tight, as my independence and lifestyle were costly.

Contracts ended.

Redundancies were rife.

Friends and family had their own lives to lead.

Loneliness seeped in.

Fear of losing my home threatened.

Jobs were unfulfilling.

I was now having to take on additional work to make ends meet.

I didn't always have enough to eat and bills were a constant pressure.

With no-one to turn to, (because of pride), I battled on, but felt that I was often on the losing side.

There was no-one close enough to me for my struggle to be revealed.

I continued on as though all was well, but I knew the opposite was true.

At this point, God began to reveal Himself to me.

In hindsight this was apparent, but at the time I could neither identify nor explain it.

As I continued down my path, God would intervene and prevent me from making some terrible choices – however, some, He permitted.

I know now that I needed to learn from those mistakes, but, at the time I questioned the meaning of life.

Of course, I recognise now, that this was a good thing, as it led me to Him, but back then I struggled to understand why life was so unjust.

Soon, after this period of wondering in a dark and lonely wilderness, God took hold of me, and I committed to Him, and life began to turn around for me.

But, here I was again, in a very different way, feeling out of control and – if I'm honest – a little afraid.

My new understanding of relationships was that it was a lifetime commitment, with divorce not being an option.

I'll be very honest with you – I struggled with this concept.

My life plan had been to do what I saw others do in my lifetime – including my own parents. Marry, have children (not necessarily in that order), then get divorced when it got tough or he cheated, or both!

I hadn't stopped to consider any alternatives to this plan.

It was my safety net, and I was running with it.

I can't recall exactly when I heard the new, revised plan (divorce not being an option), but it was within a matter of weeks of giving my life to Christ. Well, as you can imagine, this blew my mind.

I just couldn't conceive it!

I didn't know what the alternative looked like.

It was as if someone – namely, my senior pastor, was leading me into no-man's land, with a blindfold, ear plugs in and my hands bound behind my back!

I needed to know more.

I plunged into the word of God.

Matthew, Mark, Exodus....they all confirmed what Pastor Steve had just taught me.

Contradictorily, I felt fearful yet comforted all at the same time.

Fearful, because my understanding, as well as my future plan, had just been challenged, and, well, shattered.

However, comforted that I was now being guided, as I never had before.

I felt like I was no longer just 'making my way through life' but I now had guidance.

A rule to follow, if you like.

Something concrete.

I won't lie to you – I was also comforted by the exception to the rule in Matthew 19 verse 9.

Whilst I wasn't looking for an escape route, my exposure to infidelity whilst growing up and then experiencing it directly in my own relationships meant that I was particularly sensitive in this area.

Throughout the years to follow, five years to be exact, God worked a small miracle in me to prepare me for my blessing, namely Rob.

And here I was agreeing to do life together with him and suddenly I felt .... vulnerable!

This was real.

Surreal.

It was happening, and I was scared, ecstatic, elated, nervous, wobbly, thrilled, cautious, wary, excited......all of the above.

7 FULL STEAM AHEAD

So, Rob and I agreed that we were entering into a romantic relationship but neither of us really knew what that looked like. Rob had had relationships since becoming a Christian, but he confesses with his own lips that he had not conducted himself in a Godly fashion whilst in those relationships.

In fact, Rob had come to a point in his life where he had given up on having a successful relationship – And, he takes full responsibility for the downfall of those relationships.

In one heated moment with God, Rob declared, "That's it God! I'm done with women!

From now on, it's just you and me!" And he meant it.

Two weeks later, at the Church Weekend Away I'm calling him over to me and telling him, 'I need to find you a wife!'

Rob was scared.

He didn't want to mess this one up.

I was scared.

I wasn't sure how to do this. I didn't know how to let my guard down.

We were both experiencing feelings that felt way beyond what we had felt before, but we couldn't tell anyone.

I was on my knees before God constantly – asking God to remove him or remove me – '*send me on a mission Lord*', I pleaded, '*just don't let my heart get involved with this man if he is not to be my husband!*'

Dramatic! I know. But it's the truth.

I really was afraid of feeling what I was feeling and then having it removed.

Rob, on the other hand, was 'sprung!' He confesses this.

He just couldn't understand how he could feel what he was feeling, so quickly, and without having had sex.

That's the truth!

It confused and scared him.

Remember, this was all happening within two weeks of first speaking to each other.

To add to the emotions we were already feeling, we were both in awe of each other - but for different reasons.

On my part, I didn't feel worthy of Rob because he was 'mister nice guy'. Anyone who spoke of Rob held him is such high regard. Auntie's loved him, young people admired and respected him.

At the mention of Rob's name, heads would tip to one side and eyes would become doughy.

No-one thought of me that way!

I was thought of as strong, tough, blunt......you get the picture.

Rob's feeling of unworthiness came from my involvement within the church. I had thrown myself into so much activity that I had quite a visual presence, especially on a Sunday. I could often be seen pacing up and down the aisles, resolving issues, operating the media desk, and so on.

Rob thought I was someone of importance and responsibility within the church and didn't feel he could 'step to me'.

His words.

In addition, neither of us had the physical qualities that the other would ordinarily have looked for in a desired partner.

So, in short, we would not have chosen each other, in the natural.

But in the Spirit, God was at work. He had removed the veil and we could now see each other spiritually.

The day following the telephone call, and, having made the decision to progress our relationship I was due to visit IKEA to purchase items for an upcoming church event. Rob was due to play football, as he did, every Saturday morning. He had already advised me that the game always took place, irrespective of the weather.

It was December and it was wet and cold.

I asked him, on the Friday night, whether the game would still go ahead due to the freezing temperature. He told me that the only reason a game would be cancelled due to weather, is if the pitch had become water logged – which never, ever happens.

Saturday morning, I arose.

I decided to text Rob, just to say, 'Good morning', like you do.

Rob calls me immediately and tells me that the football match is cancelled as the pitch is water logged.

Mmmmm! Like....what on.........

We agree to meet up and go to IKEA together. We wanted to spend time together.

Whilst there, the irony was not wasted on me.

All those trips to IKEA as a single woman. Now, here I am........but, it's early days.

IKEA accomplished, we agree to go for drinks.

We want to stay together.

We get hungry. We go for a meal.

Chinese.

We are not ready to part ways.

We arrange to see a movie, a bit later, in the evening.

We part ways.

Briefly.

I meet Rob at his sister's place, later.

He invites me in to meet her.

A first for Rob.

I wasn't expecting that.

She's lovely. Welcoming.

We leave for the cinema, and we are chatting away.

It's easy.

I choose the movie.

I regret it.

It has profanity and sexual scenes right from the beginning despite being rated a 12A.

I'm embarrassed.

I don't even look at Rob to investigate how he is feeling.

I'm too embarrassed.

The sex scene is followed by a funeral scene.

As I mentioned earlier, Rob's mum passed away just the month before.

I'm frustrated with myself.

I wasn't to know, but no matter.

This time, I look at Rob. He seems okay.

I want to hold his hand. To console him. I feel bad for him.

I don't dare.

He will think I'm too 'forward'.

I watch the screen but I'm not really seeing.

I start to fidget.

So does Rob.

Something's happening.

Rob is leaning on his hand which is against his face, elbow propped on the armrest which we share.

He looks uncomfortable, troubled......it's hard to tell.

I take his hand.

Fire shoots up my arm as our fingers interlock. Like, a tingly but fierce heat, that reaches my shoulder, and goes no further, but the burn continues.

I grip Rob's hand.

I close my eyes, and.......I pray!

I am actually sitting in the cinema, praying, silently. No lip movement but praying in my head.

I have no idea at the time, but Rob is experiencing exactly the same thing. He is praying too.

The movie ends.

We leave in silence.

We drive home, in silence, and part ways, exchanging polite farewells, but nothing more.

Sunday arrives.

I am on the front row at church, crying out to God. Literally crying. I desperately need Him to tell me that Rob is the one and it is all going to be okay. Despite the feelings and the ease of being with Rob I want to know for sure – and only God can tell me. But I can't hear Him.

At the end of the service, the same auntie that has been praying with me for the past three years regarding my 'help mate' comes to find me, and tells me that, God has told her to tell me, to 'be at peace'. She gives me the scripture, John 14:27, and tells me that our season of praying and fasting is complete.

She hugs me, tight.

She smiles a knowing smile and she walks away.

Job done.

Over the next couple of weeks Rob and I spend a lot of time talking and a lot of time with God. We see a lot of each other and talk about me being his wife and him being my husband begins to creep into our conversations.

We didn't tell anyone about our relationship.

On my part, I was still consulting with God. I didn't want anyone else's input at that stage.

I knew that Rob was a 'nice guy'; I was discovering that for myself. But, I didn't want that to sway my focus. Being a nice guy was one thing. But was that 'nice guy' *my* husband? Or someone else's?

I wasn't prepared to risk falling into that trap.

I remained very prayerful.

I wasn't asking God to make him my husband – quite the opposite. I was asking God to remove him if he wasn't.

Two weeks into dating, we agree to go and see Pastor Steve. Neither of us wanted to invest any further if it wasn't to be.

Now, hear my heart.

It was not for pastor Steve to decide whether we were to be together, or not.

That was God's job.

But, as our leader and shepherd we were accountable to him and we valued his spiritual input. He knew us both and had watched us develop throughout our time at his church. So, we valued his opinion and submitted to his authority.

"Share it!" he told us.

Having had my initial life plan drastically altered by understanding that divorce was no longer an option, I had created a new plan.

I have already explained that I am a planner, an organiser, a forward thinker, and so, I find it difficult to operate without a plan of some sort.

My new, revised life-plan, with regards to relationships and marriage, looked something like this;

Meet someone.

Date for at least two years.

Be engaged for 18 months.

Plan our wedding – 18 months

Get married after having been with the person for approx. 5 years in total.

God had other plans.

As Rob stood up to give his speech on our wedding day, he said these words, *"If anyone had told me, I would be standing here, on my wedding day, after only 11 months of dating, I would say, "You are crazy!"*

And, I agreed with him.

Only God could have made that happen in either one of our lives.

We had both come from divorced homes with absent fathers whom we visited occasionally.

We had both come from all female homes with elder sisters and mum at home – no male example.

We were both youngest children – used to being dictated to by older siblings but a little spoilt by mum.

Neither of us had had a burning desire to be married.

Neither of us had been in relationships that had lasted much more than 4-6 months.

Lifetime commitments to another person was, pretty much, alien to us both.

But God.

8 SIDE BY SIDE

As we entered married life, Rob & I quickly learned some truths – about ourselves, and each other.

We floated through our honeymoon, starry-eyed and caught up in the wonderment of companionship, freedom and sex.

Our idyllic surroundings set the backdrop for a dreamy escape from all the hectic planning and purchasing that had been our lives for the previous four months.

We relaxed, and we enjoyed each other.

There was not one iota of reality during that two-week period.

We travelled well and considered each other thoughtfully throughout our two-part honeymoon.

We married in early December so arriving home from honeymoon during the Christmas season meant we hit the ground running.

I went immediately back to work as well as taking on the usual preparations for the season.

What we hadn't anticipated was the two of us falling ill almost immediately, which wiped us out. As flu gripped the both of us, and with no actual bed to sleep in, memories of our honeymoon paradise were all but forgotten.

Small cracks started to appear.

Despite both living alone prior to being married, Rob and I had not stayed at each other's houses. We had not holidayed together.

Although we had spent time together, pretty much every day, we had not been in each other's space for extended periods of time.

If we had to go back to that period, we would not change it.

I *loved* the fact that my first holiday with Rob was our honeymoon.

I *loved* the fact that the first time we woke up together in the morning was the day after our wedding.

I *loved* the fact that we had not explored each other sexually until our wedding night.

I wouldn't change any of it.

But.

Our stubbornness, independence, feistiness and the voices of our respective mothers reverberating in our memory banks, meant that we started to lock horns on occasion.

And, those occasions, started to increase in frequency.

A few months into marriage, we had a raging argument.

I have absolutely no idea what the argument was about or how it started.

I remember being in the lounge.

We were arguing.

I got up and stormed out of the room, slamming the door.

I stomped all the way to the bedroom at the other end of the hallway and slammed that door too.

I thrust myself onto the bed, raging.

I listened.

Nothing.

I waited.

Still nothing.

My spirit is telling me to pray. To talk to God.

My head is saying, "No!"

My head wins.

Even angrier now, I rip the bedroom door open, stomp back to the lounge, thrust that door open and glare at Rob.

"DON'T YOU EVEN CARE THAT I HAVE JUST LEFT THIS ROOM ANGRY AND UPSET?" I shouted.

Rob, calmly, as if in slow motion, looked up from the newspaper he was reading, turned to face me and said matter of factly, "I didn't send you anywhere." Followed by, "When you are ready...to come and talk...like a civilized human being...I'll be right here." And, with that, he turned another page of the newspaper.

I was livid!

But, I had no comeback.

I felt unbelievably foolish.

Chastised like a child.

Powerless to do anything.

On repeat - I turned on my heels, slammed the lounge door, stomped back to the bedroom, slammed that door, thrust myself onto the bed.......and stayed there.

Raging. Again.

I thought about leaving the flat. But where would I go?

I thought about sitting in the car.

Cold.

Friends or family were out of the question. I didn't want anyone to know that I had argued with Rob and I'm not good at pretending all is well when it really isn't.

Only a couple of months ago we had stood before these very people looking starry eyed, declaring our love for one another. I couldn't let them know that all was not well.

A seed of doubt was sown.

My mind was now wondering whether I'd done the right thing.

A rollercoaster of thoughts and emotions were chasing through my mind.

I felt out of control.

I'm a control freak!

But I couldn't control Rob.

I didn't think I wanted to control Rob but at this moment I had built several scenarios in my head and he wasn't acting out any of them. At least five of the scenarios involved him walking into the bedroom and attempting to make peace.

One of them involved him swooping into the room, door flung wide, pausing to take in the sight of me, sad and sorrowful on our bed, leaning in toward me with arms outstretched, grabbing me in his arms and telling me firmly and forcefully that he loved me, and he hated when we argued........

I didn't marry *that* man.

I hear him coming down the hallway.

Finally.

I compose myself.

He doesn't enter the bedroom.

I listen.

He is in the spare bedroom next door.

I can hear movement and the wardrobe being opened.

Huh?

HE IS NOT TRYING TO PACK AND LEAVE ME??!!?

As I listen intently for more clues, I can't fathom what is happening.

The bedroom door opens.

"I'm going shop. D'you want anything?" he asks. He doesn't sound or look angry, but there's no love in his voice either. Just neutral tones.

I am aghast with disbelief.

I want to say, "Are you serious?" Followed by, "Your WIFE is sitting here, broken and hurting, not knowing which way to turn or whether there is actually any future in this so-called marriage, and you are asking me if I want anything from the SHOP!!!!"

I don't.

I say, "No."

He leaves.

I'm furious. Even more so.

There is nothing I can do.

I had never felt so powerless with regards to my own environment.

In previous relationships I would have walked away. Never to return.

My mind is working overtime, thinking of what to do next.

I feel trapped.

I could go. Just to worry him. But I'd have to return – at least to collect my things.

And go where?

I'm staying.

I.....don't......know......what......to....do!!!

Rob returns from the shop.

He doesn't come into the bedroom.

I hear the lounge door close, softly.

Can he not even offer me the courtesy of displaying some anger?

I hear nothing.

Hold on.... I hear something....

Football!

HE IS ACTUALLY WATCHING A MATCH!!!

I cannot believe this!

Where am I on this man's list of priorities?

I desperately want to go and see what he is doing.

What did he get from the shop?

I'm hungry.

I can't.

I feel stupid.

I stay put.

I wake up.

It's early.

Rob is asleep next to me.

I'm still angry.

I'm extremely hungry.

I go to the lounge. No sign of what Rob did in my absence last night.

I go to the kitchen. To the fridge. I'll have some cereal.

I reach for the milk.

Wine.

WINE!!!

He went to the shop to get WINE!

I was in complete torment last night.... raging, hurting, isolated....

And he was drinking wine, watching a match, flicking pages of the newspaper.

My head wants to burst.

Sod the cereal.

This man is taking the mick!

Rob is up now.

I want this dealt with. Now!

I confront him.

Right there, in the hallway – face to face.

I rant.... on and on, about him not caring whether I was upset and not wanting to sort things out. I express my feelings about him chilling on the sofa with wine and Arsenal whilst I am curled up on the bed in torment. I rage about wanting to walk out of the door and question whether he would even care or even NOTICE if I left.

I really went there.

Rob took in everything I said and then he opened his mouth.

Tornado!

He kept it short, but it was *not* sweet.

In a nutshell, he blasted, "WHO DO YOU WANT ME TO BE?" "IS ANYTHING I DO GOOD ENOUGH?"

And, with that, he walked to the lounge and sat on the sofa, head in hands.

I followed, after a pause.

I stood in the doorway and looked at him.

What had I done?

I was breaking him.

I walked over to him.

Took his hands.

Pulled him to standing.

And, hugged him.

He hugged me back.

Never again.

I had learned a valuable lesson.

In trying to control my environment, I was breaking my leader.

I didn't want him broken.

I had spent years praying for someone that was whole.

Was I now going to be the one that broke him? I was supposed to be his help-mate, his cheerleader, his confidant. I was supposed to respect him and honour him and encourage him and be there for him if he fell or failed.

I was not supposed to be the one that caused him to fall or fail.

I vowed to never repeat that behaviour - and I meant it.

But I was missing something.

9 ON THE WRONG TRACK

As we continued our journey there were many changes. Because the first house we had chosen for married life had 'fallen through' a month or so before our wedding, we had made the decision to rent, on the premise that it would only be for 6-12 months.

We were blessed to have the deposit we needed for our first home, so we didn't want to rent for too long. We wanted to take the time to find the right house for our new life together, so we rented a lovely flat whilst we took our time to view a multitude of properties in the quest to find 'the one' for us.

We quickly discovered that we loved looking at properties and discussing our views, the likes and the dislikes, the minute we got back into our car.

We viewed so many properties, but few with the right fit and feel for us.

One afternoon, we looked at a three-bedroom semi-detached house in a quiet cul-de-sac and we knew it was the one. We saw beyond the doggy smell and the yellow and green walls and knew we could build a home and start our family there.

As we stepped out of the property, thanking the vendor for showing us around, we didn't even wait to get to our car. We gave each other 'the look' – this was the one.

Leaving our first married home, even though it was temporary, was a little hard for me. I'd loved it there.

I had owned many properties and lived in a number of places but this one held a special place in my heart. Rob and I had great memories of finding the flat by chance and me moving in four days before our wedding. Pre-wedding photos of me getting ready for the ceremony with my bridesmaids and Uncle Fruits (I'll explain later) were all taken in that flat.

Rob and I had decided not to bring any furniture from our respective homes when we got married so we had no furniture when we initially moved in, after the honeymoon.

No bed, no sofa, nothing. Only our personal items –books, clothes, etc, came with us. Everything else belonged to our pasts.

Two weeks after returning from honeymoon, having slept on blankets on the floor, we purchased a mattress, but we had to wait another four weeks for our bed to arrive and an additional two weeks for the sofa to arrive.

It had all been worth it.

As we built our lives together the excitement and wonder carried us through – even the tougher times.

As we settled in to our new place we started to appreciate the freedom of ownership and we got to work making changes and personalising our space to reflect us and our vision for our future.

Soon after we moved in, I flew out to the Philippines on a mission trip. Rob continued to work on our home and I was excited to return and see what changes he had made. It was an exciting time and every day held an opportunity for us to put our stamp on our new season.

However, during that time, a challenge we had not had to face before presented itself and we were not at all sure how to deal with it.

A few months prior, we had made the decision to start trying for children. By now, I was 33 and we had always expressed the desire for a family with more than one or even two children.

I had shared with Rob that I would like a bit of time with just the two of us – maybe some travel time also, but the reality of age and circumstance were presenting themselves and we agreed to start preparing for our family to grow.

By the time we moved into our second married home we had already been trying for quite a few months and we were not conceiving. We understood that these things take time, but each month was a reminder that our desire was not being fulfilled.

As things settled down and the decorating was completed we got into the routine of daily life. By now I was working for our church and that brought its own challenges. I had a lot to learn.

Planning, organisation and administration came naturally to me, but I had to learn about ministry.

I had come from a corporate background, so it took a while to adjust to how things were done – not only locally but as a charity. Largely, the main challenge came from working and worshipping in the same place. I quickly realised that I was never 'off duty', so to speak.

Wherever I went someone was greeting me, knowing me by name and asking about Rob. This threw me as I wouldn't always be able to identify them.

It made sense, as part of my role was to give the announcements of events and suchlike at the Sunday services and so, visually, I was known by many in the church. But of course, I didn't always know them. It's a large church!

Working for a church was not at all what I expected it to be. I expected it to be tranquil, peaceful, and populated with saints that floated through the corridors casting blessings over all those who passed their way.

In reality, this was not the case. It was busy, often hectic, and sometimes fraught with tension. With a small staff base covering a broad spectrum of duties, no day was ever dull.

Rob also worked locally so we would drive in to work, and home again, together. Initially, this was wonderful. A great opportunity to talk to each other about our day or make plans for the day.

But gradually the pressures of work took their toll. Any frustration, from either of us, was vented on the way home from work.

If I was not ready to leave when Rob came to collect me from work – tension.

If Rob was held up at work and left me waiting – tension.

The grace was evaporating.

Coupled with the pressure of not conceiving and the absence of the initial excitement of marriage and building our home, we found ourselves struggling to enjoy the very thing we had longed for when we first came together.

During this period, we had the worst fight we've ever had in our marriage.

Again, I have no recollection of what caused the argument, but the outcome was, Rob and I did not speak to each other for a whole week!

Not one word.

No greetings – nothing.

I would awake super early and leave the house for work before Rob would arise.

There was no communication throughout the day and I would find alternative things to do so as not to return home until late.

On arrival at home, if Rob was in the lounge I would head straight up to the bedroom and get myself off to sleep. If Rob was in the bedroom, when I got home I would stay downstairs until I could hear the familiar sounds of Rob sleeping, then I would crawl, quietly into bed.

Rob would do the same and we operated around each other like this for the whole week.

Neither of us was prepared to cave – as though we were marking our territory.

At this point we did not have a car and so it was easier to head out for the train station without having to wait for each other. We both invented ways of being out of the house so as not to cross paths in the evenings.

It was awful.

I began to feel that the very reason I had not wanted to get married – or stay married – was now upon me.

Things were getting very difficult between Rob and I and we didn't know where to turn. We were both unsure about speaking to anyone or asking for help.

We tried our best to paint the pretty picture for those around us, but the reality was, we were struggling.

10 DERAILED

After what we now refer to as, 'our week of silence', Rob and I began to speak again.

We were both still angry and neither of us wanted to 'give', but we were exhausted with the effort of avoiding each other.

Our reconciliation started with angry, one liners – but, determined to put an end to the dreadful, emotional torture, we both pushed through the anger and began to talk.

We vowed that we would never, ever get to that place again.

And we haven't.

But, all was not well.

We had still not conceived, and despite being prayerful, fasting and even taking the bold step of decorating the 3rd bedroom as a nursery, there was still no baby.

We agreed, it was time to get professional help.

By now, we had been trying for a year and I was now 34. I was fully aware of the risks of conceiving after 35 but we had rejected those statistics and believed that God would give us healthy babies.

Plural.

"We normally wait until you have been trying for two years before we do any further investigations."

My GP was frustrating me.

"Doctor", I said, with as much patience as I could muster, "I am 34 years old. I do not HAVE TIME, to wait another year, to THEN be told that there is an issue. I would prefer to know NOW, so that we can do something about it."

The doctor could see the tension building within me.

He was being dismissive.

What I needed was encouragement, direction, guidance.

And answers.

As he handed me a sample bottle, he gave me instructions and dismissed me from his office.

I'll be honest, I snatched the bottle and left.

On Monday morning I returned the sample bottle to the GP reception and left with instructions to call back three days later for the results.

I tried to put it out of my mind, but memories of a previous doctor's report kept replaying in my head.

Months before, Rob and I had been to see another doctor who had asked Rob to do a sperm sample. As we had sat, to hear the results, we were fairly relaxed. I guess you could say we were more curious than worried.

"Mr Harris, you have a low sperm count. Which means the probability of you conceiving children is drastically lowered and may not happen at all. You can make changes to your lifestyle in an effort to assist

with conception, but the chances will still remain very low."

We left that doctors surgery, and as we walked to our car, Rob looked at me, I looked at him and he just shrugged his shoulders.

Without words, he was telling me, 'God is in control'.

Later that evening, Rob asked me, "Whose report are we going to believe, the doctors report or God's report?"

We chose to believe God's report.

Thursday afternoon, as I wait on hold to hear the result of my requested sample, the line clicks as the receptionist takes me off hold.

"I'm sorry Mrs Harris......."

My heart sinks.

My eyes close.

She continues, "......the results have not come back from the lab yet. Please call again tomorrow."

Click.

In that second, with my emotions all over the place, I make the decision.

I'm buying a test on the way home and I'm doing it, with Rob, tonight.

I cannot, will not, wait another day.

I call Rob.

He agrees.

That evening we do the test.

It's positive!

We're having a baby!

Despite being elated about our news, our struggles continued.

We weren't constantly arguing but things were not joyful in our household. We were rolling along and being amicable.

There were up days, and there were down days, and then there were days somewhere in between.

We muddled along and tried to focus on the excitement of having a baby – something we had both wanted – so much.

In the midst of all that was going on, we received a call from a couple that ran the relationship ministry at our church.

We had attended the pre-marriage course in preparation for our own marriage and had found it incredibly useful and informative.

The course was a requirement for any couple wanting to get married at our church and we were excited to attend it at the time.

We enjoyed the topics and discussions and the interaction with other couples and after the 6th and final session we felt we had learned so much. There were a few other couples who were already married that came and shared their experiences of marriage with us all. It was enlightening and somewhat eye-opening.

These couples were very real and open about their own challenges and it helped us to be open too.

When we received the call, we were curious as to why they would be calling us.

We were asked whether we would like to come and assist on the course and generally help out with refreshments, laying out of chairs, etc.

We discussed it with each other and agreed that we would like to get involved in whatever capacity.

However, we weren't sure we would have much to contribute as we were not really in the best place within our own marriage.

We prayed and asked God whether this was His plan for us.

We both felt that God was directing us toward this ministry, and so, we accepted and went along.

That was our turning point.

11 MISSION CONTROL

As previously explained, neither Rob nor I had experienced good examples of marriage growing up. Neither of us had experienced good, healthy relationships of our own during our own dating experiences.

We both discovered the truth about marriage as we became Christians.

Understanding that divorce was not an option and that the wedding vows were not just lovely, rhythmic, poetic words that were declared for your friends and family on your wedding day meant that we were constantly looking for guidance and good examples to follow.

Honestly, we didn't see many great examples around us in those early days. Apart from the pre-marriage course that we attended where the focus was entirely on preparation for marriage – we could count on one hand the marriages we observed around us that we could admire.

We really needed some role models that we could learn from so we decided it would be a good idea to take up the offer to assist with the relationship ministry and glean from the leaders.

As we attended the pre-marriage course for the second time – now married and with a different perspective – we started to see the teaching in a different, more applicable way.

As the leaders asked the attendees to *'highlight four things that attracted them to their partner'*, Rob and I decided to take part in the exercise too.

As I told Rob what attracted me to him, I felt a fraction of my tension toward him fall away. As he told me what attracted him to me, my eyes moistened a little.

We hadn't said this stuff to each other for a couple of years.

We needed it.

As the course continued, and as we took part in the exercises, conversations and discussions, we began to restore the feelings we had once shown each other in abundance.

An excitement was building within us – but it wasn't just for our own relationship.

Something bigger was growing.

A planted seed was being watered.

And now there were shoots surfacing.

The ministry leaders were inspiring – they shared, so openly, about their own marriage.

They invited us in to the highs and lows of the marriage relationship and they gave it all a reality that was tangible.

Historically, I had either heard, 'Marriage is hard work' or 'Marriage is wonderful'.

Honestly, more of the former and not so much of the latter.

But, the pre-marriage course was giving us a combination of both that was achievable and successful and, dare I say it, enjoyable.

We came away at the end of the final session feeling that we had had marriage therapy.

The future began to look like there was a possibility that we could actually make marriage work.

As our pregnancy progressed, we had more to focus on than just our own needs and wants.

We began to prepare for our child to arrive into our world.

Rob was elated about becoming a father and often couldn't contain it. I loved seeing him so excited.

I was also delighted, but, there was an element of apprehension.

Remember, I'm a planner.

Thinking about the birth and arrival of our child, also had me thinking about the life changes that would occur.

Work. Pause.

Freedom. Pause.

Sleep. Pause.

Travel and holidays. Pause.

Shopping (did I mention, I LOVE shopping?) Pause.

Size 10. Pause.

Of course, I also considered all the wonderful things that motherhood would bring, but I couldn't help feeling that life would never be the same again.

And I was right.

As our first son was introduced to our growing family, life adjusted drastically.

He was wonderful. A real delight.

And motherhood, in itself, wasn't as difficult as the books and magazines depicted. Not in the practical sense anyway. Initially, our son would feed and then sleep for four hours (during the day), giving me plenty of time to clean, cook etc. But, of course, he would wake through the night wanting to be fed.

My struggle was my lack of independence, isolation, lack of money and generally not being able to do what I wanted to do when I wanted to do it.

As time passed, with just a few weeks passed since his birth, our baby was dictating my every move – from when I slept, to when I showered or brushed my teeth. Even going to the toilet was a planned mission with limited timeframes.

After three months I was desperate to go back to work.

Again, our relationship was affected.

I resented Rob for getting up every morning – at a time set by his alarm (not a screaming baby), having a shower (without the pressure of a screaming baby on the other side of the door), brushing his teeth (without the pressure of a screaming baby on the other side of the door), getting dressed (into clothes that actually fit him) (without the pressure of a screaming baby on the other side of the door) *swanning* off in the car (without the pressure of a screaming baby in the seat next to him) and chatting with his colleagues all day long, with a peaceful, uninterrupted break for lunch every day (without a screaming baby in a bouncy chair at his feet) with the occasional visit to the gym (let's not even go there!!!)

I would go for long walks with our son in his pushchair just to pass the time most days but internally I was really struggling.

I had nothing to plan or prepare for.

Everyday felt the same.

I tried visiting friends, but with a baby in tow, conversation, meaningful conversation was a real struggle.

Enough!

I cut my 'year off' short and made plans to go back to work.

When our son was seven months old I returned to work.

I worked full-time and juggled motherhood.

I enjoyed it.

I got tired.

But I felt purposeful.

Being back at work meant more involvement in church activity and the relationship ministry continued to be our lifeline. It grounded us and reminded us of our purpose for being married in the first place.

One of the sessions covered on the pre-marriage course was 'Children', and now we had our own child, that too had become our reality.

It also reminded us of our vision to have more than one child. Our plan, even before conceiving our first child, was to have our 2nd child in quick succession of the first. My age was a major factor in this but we also both liked the idea of having our children close in age. Of course, we were mindful of the difficulty we had in conceiving the first time around, so we took no precautions after our first son was born and one year and nine months after we had our first son, our second son was born.

In contrast to our first son who was pretty laid back and tranquil, our second son was active, vocal and never seemed to stop moving.

He hasn't changed.

With the arrival of this new addition to our family came the major decision of me not returning to work.

With a new-born and a one year old, nursery fees were crippling, and energy levels were dwindling.

I stayed home with the children while Rob worked multiple jobs to keep the roof over our heads.

Rob is a visionary and an optimist.

His decision to purchase a four-bedroom house when we had one child meant that we weren't forced to move as our family expanded but it also meant a rather large mortgage repayment every month.

Not to mention the heating bill.

But, that aside, Rob worked extremely hard to support his growing family and he thrived in fatherhood.

I continued to struggle at times but with two very young children to care for, boredom was no longer an issue.

My mind, however, continued to search for alternative activity.

12 ACTUALLY.... I DO!

I had always wanted to be a mother and I felt confident that I could be a great mother.

The reality was quite unexpected.

Motherhood brought out many sides of me. Some, as I said, were quite unexpected.

I always knew that I liked my own space and my freedom, but until it was forcefully removed from me, I didn't appreciate just how much of it I'd had.

Marriage had imposed certain limitations, but I was happy to go along with those, after all, being respectful and courteous to my husband by telling him where I was and what time I'd be home was an adjustment I was more than willing to make.

But motherhood, that was a whole other dimension.

At times, I wanted to scream, or run, or hide, or cry, or stay in the shower with the hot water pouring over me, forever.

I felt forced to function.

Forced to respond.

Quickly.

Nothing could wait anymore.

But, having said all that, at the same time, paradoxically, I was finding my groove as a wife and mother.

I was resisting less and accepting more.

Rob would often 'take over' with the children when he came home from work and suggest I take some time out.

I appreciated this so much that it made me want to serve him more.

In Rob, I saw a man who loved his family, who worked hard to provide for us, who never complained about working three jobs, who listened when I chatted endlessly about my day, despite being tired, who slept sitting up in bed because one of his sons had fallen asleep on his chest and he didn't want to disturb them. Who ate fish and chips some nights because I didn't have the energy to cook, again.

The focus, for both of us, became......us.

Allowing someone to take care of me, even my own husband, was an alien concept that I had little experience with.

My mother, as I said, sacrificed so much to take care of her children. And somewhat selfishly, I had expected her to. Not realising, until I became a mother myself, just how endless and selfless her life had been.

My first, adult experience of being looked after and cared for, by someone who did not have the parental or spousal duty to do so, came in the unusual form of Uncle Fruits.

Do you remember, much earlier on, I mentioned the elderly man, with the white hair and the goatee that shook my hand as I entered the church for the first time?

Well, that very dear uncle was a pillar of strength and support to me from the very beginning of my journey with Christ.

His real name was, of course, not Uncle Fruits, but that was my name for him and here's why.

As I began my journey in Christ and I attended church every Sunday and often throughout the week Uncle Fruits began his process of adoption.

Months after I started attending the church I had a fall and broke my ankle which left me in a cast, and on crutches, for eight weeks. I would hobble into church and would sit with my right leg raised at the front of the church whilst worship took place followed by the sermon.

Uncle Fruits later told me that that is when God really laid me on his heart and he began to pray for me regularly. One day, soon after my accident, at the beginning of the Sunday service, Uncle Fruits brought me a carrier bag laden with fruit.

Mangoes, strawberries, pears and oranges.

He handed me that bag and said, "This is for you. Enjoy." And he walked away with a knowing look on his face and a smirk in his smile.

He knew.

He knew that I was often struggling to eat at that period in my life.

My income didn't always stretch to food supplies, so I ate what I could at work – leftovers from the corporate lunches and giveaways and promotions from the local eateries.

He knew my need.

God had shown him.

Every week, without fail, before or after the service, Uncle Fruits handed me that bag.

That bag would feed me when there was nothing else.

Every week, until I got married.

Every week, for four years.

Over two HUNDRED bags of fruit.

Without fail.

As I walked down the aisle on my wedding day, towards my future husband, holding on to the arm of the man that had fed me fruit, I was being handed over.

Mission accomplished.

Years later, I lay a wreath made of fruit on the grave of Uncle Fruits.

I stepped back.

I didn't have tears of sadness in my eyes.

We had said our goodbyes and he had left me with an abundance of wisdom and guidance.

I had a smile of joy and the smell of mangoes to remind me of the great man that had cared for me. In my arms I had the white roses that he had instructed someone to give to me after he had parted. She handed them to me at his funeral and although I sobbed outwardly, internally I smiled. Even in death, he remained the distinguished gentleman I had seen that first day when I entered the church building.

Uncle Fruits.

Rob and I pressed on, caring for our sons and each other.

In the difficult times, we encouraged each other and sometimes in the silences we understood without saying a word.

I took on part time, evening work so that Rob could rest a bit more and spend time with his sons. I didn't enjoy my work much, but I felt purposeful and I was able to be me again for a few hours each day. I also enjoyed contributing to the household income.

During this season, our 3rd son was born. Our family was rapidly expanding, and God saw fit to add even more 'sons' to our swelling family.

Stephane and Gavin, both with their own sons, came to be a part of our family and lived with us for a period of time. One was planned, the other wasn't, as such, but both were a wonderful, God ordained, addition to our family.

Our marriage was now under a microscope.

Unintentionally, we were being watched and observed.

Not by condemning eyes. Not in judgement. We, as a married couple, were curious to them all.

Our natural, birth sons were experiencing life for the first time and learning about the varying concepts of family life. They were recognising that not all families were the same. As they attended school or church and as they made friends it was dawning on them that different children had differing circumstances and environments from which they came.

Gavin and Stephane had not come from stable family backgrounds, much like myself and Rob, and therefore, they watched. And they listened. And they asked.

It was wonderful to have them in our family.

They were our family.

Having a house full of sons confirmed a word God had given Rob years before.

'A Father to the Fatherless.'

Rob was already working with young people and had been for years. He was influential in his work and made a real impact in the lives of many. But, now he was living in a home surround by sons, natural and spiritual, and God was moulding him for what was to come.

As for me.

I was growing.

13 WHAT'S IN YOUR HAND?

As time went on, there were so many changes and adjustments being made that I had learned to let go and let God.

It wasn't easy and sometimes I put up a fight, but eventually I gave in to God.

The more I saw His hand at work in our lives, the more I learned to trust Him. My faith rose, and my doubt decreased with each challenge that was thrown our way. I understood, more and more, that each season and each trial was there to strengthen us and to assist and prepare us for the next one.

I became less fearful of the challenges and more excited about what God was 'up to'.

I learnt to perceive our life and its varying climates as 'seasons'.

'Seasons' meant that nothing was permanent.

Some seasons were longer than others.

Some seasons were more enjoyable than others.

Some seasons were over far too quickly.

Some seasons seem to drag on forever.

But change kept coming.

Single to married.

Married to motherhood.

Broke to a spare fiver at the end of the month.

The changes kept us on our toes.

But I'm no ballerina!

With every change that came I learned to ask God for clarity.

I began to understand that, in every situation, big or small, I had something to learn.

In times, when I would try to get out of a situation by my own means, God would keep me right there. I would fight, not physically, of course, but mentally and emotionally I would attempt to solve, to escape, to reason – but God would not relent.

It had to be His way.

In His time.

By learning how to submit to God, and listen for his direction, I was learning to submit to my husband.

Of course, I did this the hard way.

Many times, in discussions – ok, arguments with Rob, I would know he was right. Or I knew he wanted the best for me, for us. But my flesh, my will, would not back down.

I couldn't bear the thought of being seen as weak.

I was a fighter.

I was opinionated.

I had something to say.

Always.

Silence was not something I saw as a solution.

I believed there was always something to say.

Something to contribute.

An alternative viewpoint to be shared.

God was showing me that, that was all well and good, but if I continued to talk and not listen, I would often emerge in the same spot.

Aaaargh!

It was infuriating.

But I knew He was right.

I had come to a place where I felt unsure about what God would have me do.

Generally.

In life.

I was now working from home, with a great, inspirational employer, who was both, directly and indirectly, teaching me.

Inspirational mentoring.

God had answered my prayer to be available to my family but also employed and effective outside of my home.

I didn't desire to be back in the 'rat race'.

I certainly didn't miss commuting into London or arriving home late after the children were in bed, but I was still unsure about the direction I was to take.

Since entering employment at the age of 16, I had undertaken a number of varying roles. This had helped me to eliminate the types of roles that I knew were not for me, but I was still unsure about what I was to do.

I knew my giftings.

I knew my strengths.

I knew my weaknesses.

I knew what fired me up, what I was passionate about.

I also knew my limitations, even if they were temporary.

I had been taught to not waste time trying to improve my weaknesses – but to manage them.

Agreed. I liked the sound of that.

So, what?

I became prayerful about this.

I asked God what He would have me do.

Where He would have me serve.

Do you know what He said?

'What do you have in your hand?'

Huh?

I pondered on that for a few moments – and then it came to me!

Many years before, a leader at our church had given a sermon on this very scripture. I searched for it in my bible and found it in Exodus, Chapter 4.

As Moses stood before the burning (but, not burning) bush, speaking with God, God had asked him the very same thing.

Now, don't get me wrong. I'm not claiming to be a modern-day Moses or anything.... but, I could certainly relate to this portion of scripture.

God had set before Moses a mighty task, with a huge risk and enormous responsibility. And Moses didn't feel equipped or prepared for it.

I knew nothing of my task, but reading that scripture made me nervous.

I knew that the God that I serve is; big, mighty, all powerful, ever loving, omnipotent – all of the above.

I also knew that He would use the least qualified and non-perfect people to fulfil His work here on earth.

What I didn't know at that time was how on earth (literally) He wanted to use *me*.

I had studied the likes of Moses, David, Abraham, etc. They had all 'messed up' and fallen short of the will of God in some way or another, and yet, He used them to fulfil His purposes.

I felt encouraged by this.

I didn't feel qualified, or worthy, or equipped, or even able.

But God had asked me the question.

So, I began to think about an answer.

Moses had his staff.

Basically, a big stick!

Nothing special about that!

But, see how God made it 'special'?

Not only did God show Moses what He could do with that stick, He took the time to show him, in advance, before Moses ever got near to Pharaoh.

He even went as far as to show Moses what He would do if the 'stick trick' didn't work with Pharaoh.

As I read the chapter over and over, I saw the heart of God.

My God.

My God was saying to me, 'I've got you!' 'I won't let you fall or fail.'

But I knew this came with conditions.

I knew I had to trust Him.

I had to continue to follow Him.

I had to submit to Him – first and foremost.

I always knew that God had a plan for me.

A purpose for my life.

I was taught this as a new Christian and my bible tells me so.

In that moment, my journey with Christ so far felt like.......training.

He had been holding my hand - cradling me at first, then letting me crawl, until I felt ready to stand and toddle. Now I was on my feet, He was still by my side but letting go slowly so that I could walk without being constantly aided.

I was growing up.

It was time.

Time to let me step out....in boldness....and walk forward.... towards my purpose.

But I still didn't know what my purpose was.

14 BENEATH THE SURFACE

Rob and I had become more and more involved with the relationship and marriage ministry. Having been asked to attend and serve within the ministry, we had progressed from setting out chairs and serving the lunch to contributing to the sessions and sharing our own, personal experiences.

We were then asked to lead one of the sessions. Ironically, it was the final session, which focussed on Conflict. Something we had *plenty* of experience with.

Although Rob and I had served in ministry together before, we discovered that we really had a passion for this ministry.

At the outset, we would share during the sessions and maybe speak with the couples at the end of the sessions.

Gradually, as we continued to facilitate sessions we began to get requests to meet with couples outside of these sessions. This gave us more time to really dig deeper and allow the individuals and couples to open up without the limitations of time.

We found ourselves meeting with people, one to one, more and more.

We both enjoyed these times of meeting with others and mostly we enjoyed seeing others released from previous hurts and gaining more understanding about themselves and their partner.

We got increasingly more involved and our own marriage was benefitting from the repeated teaching.

As new couples attended the course each time, we were reminded of that season of our own relationship and it revived something in us both. A renewed love, an attentiveness that had been put aside, an admiration that had become overlooked.

Annually, we would also hold a marriage conference, followed by dinner and dancing. This would awaken the planner in me and I would relish the opportunity to focus on the forthcoming event.

As we grew and gained more knowledge and experience of marriage and relationships as a whole, something became clear to us.

The teaching that was being offered to those couples who were planning for marriage was so essential. But sometimes, it was clear that, had this teaching been available prior to this stage of the relationship, there would be much less unravelling to be done at that later stage.

Worse still, much of the unravelling was happening within the marriages.

That was certainly the case for Rob and me.

I began to feel a stirring within.

What if we could have the same teaching, although somewhat adapted, for single people?

What if we could give single people the tools and knowledge to be able to make wise choices prior to being in a relationship?

What if we could help individuals to deal with their hurt, and their pain, and their shame, and their past, and their fears, their ignorance, their curiosity, their passion, their innocence, BEFORE they got into dating and relationships that would lead to marriage?

I felt an excitement in my core.

This was right.

This was needed.

This was desired by those who were struggling through relationship after relationship, not understanding what was going wrong.

I could hardly contain myself.

I spoke with the leaders of the relationship ministry and they agreed it was needed.

I spoke with my senior pastor and he agreed it was needed.

I spoke with Rob and he agreed it was needed.

So?

Where to start?

Time went by and I still hadn't progressed the idea.

Although I had 'approval' from the ministry leaders and the senior pastor a part of me was waiting to have some kind of meeting, or discussion, or something!

I spoke with Rob several times about sitting down together to start putting ideas down on paper (screen) and it just didn't materialise.

A day came when God reminded me that he had given the concept to *me*.

No-one else.

Me.

Honestly, I was a little fearful. This was unknown to me. I felt confident working with or adapting other people's material. I felt confident working with others on making their ideas come to life. I didn't feel so confident about this. This would mean starting from scratch and developing something that, to my knowledge, had not been done before in the format that was simmering in my mind.

In frustration, because Rob wasn't showing any signs of sitting down with me to do this, I sat at my computer one day and opened a blank PowerPoint slide.

I put my hands on my keyboard and I began to type.

A few weeks later the first draft of '*Rooted for Relationships*' was completed.

I had added to the work in progress every few days and it flowed so easily from me, I knew it was God.

Rob looked it over and he agreed that this was something we needed to deliver to others in the form of a teaching course.

Rob added his pearls of wisdom and we had the finished product.

We now had to decide what to do with it.

We spoke with our pastor and he agreed that we would launch the course at our church a few months later.

To say 'I was nervous' is an understatement.

But, I was also excited, expectant and elated that we had come to this point.

15 ROOTED

As we prepared to present the first course of *Rooted*, Rob and I approached the upcoming event very differently. Whilst I got busy planning the layout, décor, table centrepieces, refreshments etc, Rob appeared to be kicking back, waiting for the day to arrive. He would ask me questions and show interest but, on the whole, appeared none too fazed by the whole thing. Again, the laid-back, deal with it when it happens approach had kicked in and I was not loving it.

The platform was being prepared for yet another argument when God reminded me how this all came about in the first place.

Because of our different approaches we had experienced so much friction and frustration in our relationship. But because of that friction and frustration we now had the material for this course that was about to launch.

God reminded me that Rob and I are very different – especially in the way that we approach things. He reminded me that it took for me to let go of the idea that Rob and I would sit down together to write the material for it to ever get developed in the first place.

Whilst Rob and I contribute and operate in different ways it is that difference that makes *Rooted* what it is.

We do disagree, we do banter, we do oppose each other's ideas – sometimes in the midst of the course, for all to see. But that is who we are. That is the *real* element that allows us to *share* who we are. We present the course as a couple, side by side and so we bounce off each other.

As the day of the first course drew closer we continued to be prayerful, as, despite having the material all prepared we wanted God's plan for the course to take priority over everything else.

We watched as the bookings for attendance came in in the run up to the day and it was encouraging, very encouraging. People wanted this.

As the day came and the delegates arrived we felt at ease and the peace of God surrounded us. Rob gave me the knowing look, with the semi-smile and the narrowed eyes and we began. "Welcome......."

The feedback from that first course was very positive and we were very encouraged but more than anything we now understood why God had placed us together and why He had permitted the challenges that we had faced along the way.

Throughout our dating, we had discovered that our paths had crossed on numerous occasions long before we were in church.

Rob's best friend at the time lived adjacent to the road I grew up on. I walked along that road *every day*.

At school, I was in the same year group as his sister, Frances, and when I saw her many years later at church, I asked her what she was doing there (I hadn't seen her there before). She told me she came to witness her brother being baptised. Little did I know she would become my sister-in-law.

In my twenties, I had held a joint birthday barbecue. So many people came – Rob was one of those people – in my garden – I had no idea. We discovered this once we were married.

As I said earlier, our journey had started long before we met but God had so much work to do in both of us. Our time was not then, it was when God felt we were ready.

As we shared our journey and taught others from our own experiences and from the Word of God, we understood our initial instruction from Pastor Steve - *'Share it!'*

Each time we run the course, the Holy Spirit does something a little bit different, but the message and the question remains the same;

How can we give ourselves to others, if we don't understand who we are first?

I now know that, had I met Rob (or anyone else for that matter) prior to my encounter with God and prior to my time of preparation for marriage I could well be living in *that* house, raising my children alone and my journey in Christ would have taken a very different turn.

I certainly wouldn't be standing beside Rob delivering *Rooted* material to hundreds of people, much less writing this book.

The person I am now is recognisable yet a far cry from the person that rattled the doors of that church almost 20 years ago looking for answers.

In the area of relationships, I had so much to learn and God had to take me to a place where I was so low that I couldn't fall any further.

I don't know if that is your story, but I do know that, when it comes to relationships, especially romantic relationships that may lead to marriage, if you do not have Christ at the centre – it will be much easier to 'break'.

Though one may be overpowered by another, two can withstand him. And a threefold cord is not quickly broken.

Knowing your purpose, your calling, your mission, your path – whatever you choose to call it – will keep you focused on the plan God has for you both. Not knowing, and not asking, will have you blowing in the wind.

So, are you prepared?
Prepared to give.
Prepared to share.
Prepared to listen.
Prepared to change.
Prepared to sacrifice.
Prepared to lead.
Prepared to follow.
Prepared to submit.
Prepared to wait.
Prepared to go.

Preparation is an essential part of dating. Preparation is constant and will present itself at varying stages; some will be prepared during singleness prior to dating, some will experience this alongside your partner or spouse. Some will come in the rawest form and be prepared at later stages of marriage.

We are all being prepared, every day, all day. There is always refinement taking place, but we often resist it – because it doesn't feel good in the process. However, it is essential, and it is beneficial – to you and to your partner. Not to mention all the others around you that will benefit.

Our testimonies come from our refinement and preparation.

If you are not prepared to take a good look at yourself, why would anyone else?

If you are fearful about what you might find if you dig a little deeper into yourself, believe me, someone else is going to dig much, much, *much* deeper than you ever would.

We think of nakedness as being physically naked – without clothing.

Dating and marriage will have you naked in every other sense – emotionally, mentally, socially, spiritually, intellectually etc.

Rob has confessed to me and to hundreds of delegates attending the *Rooted* course that marriage has forced him to dig deep, deep down into areas he didn't even know existed and the process wasn't pleasurable. But the outcome and result were worth it.

I agree.

My digging started years before my marriage, but it didn't make it any easier.

But it was essential.

Every now and then, actually it would be more appropriate to say daily, God turns over my soil and weeds out my *stuff* that is not needed. He prepares my soil and plants some new seeds. Sometimes he waters the seeds that were planted a while ago.

Whichever the case, He is always at work; preparing me, uprooting me, purifying me, planting me. Sometimes he lets me rest, sometimes he demands rapid growth.

In any event, He is always there.

He does the same with Rob.

Together, with God at the centre, we equal three.

16 QUESTION?

One of the questions we ask participants of the *Rooted* course is – 'Would you date you?'

Well?

Would you?

ABOUT THE AUTHOR

Sonia Harris resides in Essex with her husband Rob and their three sons. Sonia has a passion and gifting for planning, organising and generally 'bringing order'. Outside of her commitments Sonia can be found shopping, reading, engaging in conversation, creating something or driving to or from somewhere.

If you would like to contact the author, please forward
messages to plusonesoniaharris@gmail.com

Printed in Great Britain
by Amazon